Built by Hand

Built by Hand

VERNACULAR BUILDINGS AROUND THE WORLD

Written by Athena Steen, Bill Steen,
and Eiko Komatsu

Photographs by Yoshio Komatsu

Gibbs Smith, Publisher
Salt Lake City

07 06 05 04   5 4 3 2

Published by
Gibbs Smith, Publisher
P.O. Box 667
Layton, Utah 84041

800-748-5439 orders
www.gibbs-smith.com

Edited by Madge Baird

Designed and produced by James Reyman Studio

Printed and bound in Korea

Library of Congress Cataloging-in-Publication Data

Steen, Athena Swentzell, 1961-
Built by hand / Athena Steen and Bill Steen, and Eiko Komatsu.—1st ed.
p. cm.
ISBN 1-58685-237-X
1. House construction. 2. Dwellings—Materials.
3. Vernacular architecture. 4. Architecture and society.
5. Construction industry—Appropriate technology.
I. Steen, Bill. II. Komatsu, Eiko. III. Title.
TH4811.S7 2003
728—dc21   2003000821

Contents

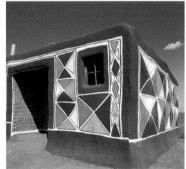

Introduction

Leaving modern architecture and its conventions far behind, Japanese photographer Yoshio Komatsu and his wife, Eiko, have traveled to some of the remotest regions on earth, compiling a stunning photographic collection of what are commonly referred to as traditional, vernacular, or indigenous buildings. Their pictures tell the story of a disappearing world of buildings that have been constructed by ordinary people who, as builders and homesteaders, have given artistic, modest, and sensible form to their daily needs and dreams. Sometimes accidental, often asymmetrical, and utilizing materials that are naturally close at hand, these buildings, with their molded curves and softened lines, convey a personal and human beauty. Quietly and almost without notice, they outwit the might of modern machinery with simple tools and materials that welcome, encourage, and amplify use of the human hand. They remind us that beauty and usefulness can come from simple things, and sometimes in ways not thought possible in today's modern consumer world. § *BUILT BY HAND* is a celebration of what is so uniquely diverse and yet similar in the buildings of different cultures around the world. It is a photographic extension of the spirit that has been portrayed in the vernacular classics: Rudofsky's *Architecture without Architects* and *The Prodigious Builders* as well as the more recent *Dwellings: The House Across the World* by Oliver. § Beginning with the most basic ways that human beings have sought shelter—beneath the trees and stars, or under the protection of a rock cliff or cave—this book traces the transformation of materials such as earth, stone, wood, and bamboo into shelters that are both stationary and movable. Doors, windows, and the connections they make between the outdoors and indoors are included, as are the marvelous and varying ways in which buildings have been decorated and embellished. We look at the solutions devised to counter climatic extremes through the use of simple devices and techniques like wind catchers, verandas, and solar orientation. The need for people to depend upon one another and their surroundings is seen through family compounds, public spaces, and villages, while the influence of cosmological beliefs and worldviews is found in the varying forms of churches, mosques, and temples. ◊ We hope that this book will bring to light the need for a modern vernacular—not the type that seeks to duplicate and imitate the examples in this book, but rather one that is inspired by a responsive and sensitive balance between the know-how and wisdom of the past and that which is sustainable and modern. The consumer-based prosperity we have experienced as a result of industrialization and science is not likely to continue at its present pace. In times to come, whether by necessity or choice, the revival and creation of that which is built by hand can serve not only to enrich our increasingly standardized lives but also to bring us back in touch with the joy that comes from people working together.

Earth

FOUND UNDERFOOT, earth has been utilized in an amazing array of methods and techniques for everything from walls to roofs to floors. It can be molded into blocks; shaped when wet into balls, coils, and the like; rammed into molds; or hand-packed into structures or frames of other materials. Extremely versatile, it combines well with many other materials, especially straw and other natural fibers.

You can decorate and sculpt with it, plaster walls with it, or use it for paint. Moldable and elastic when wet, it is capable of shapes and forms not possible with any other material. Many traditional earthen structures demonstrate remarkable aesthetic qualities that can be likened more to the art of pottery than to the uniform characteristics of conventional buildings.

In much of the world, earth has unjustly been viewed as a poor man's building material. This limited perception fails to take into account that it has been used to construct the most elegant palaces, as well as exquisite places of worship such as churches, temples, and mosques. Every type and size of house, ranging from expensive to humble, reminds us that any perceived weakness of earth as a building material can be easily overcome through a deeper understanding of traditional methods, experimentation, good design, and craftsmanship.

Interest in earth construction has grown steadily, as earth suitable for construction can be found almost everywhere in the world. It performs well in a much wider range of climates than has been previously believed. Although not a simple material

▲ FES, MOROCCO Earthen houses plastered with white clay including roofs and wood posts.

◄ KAPSIKI, CAMEROON. Mixing mud with feet.

to use well, the necessary skills and knowledge can be easily learned.

Little more than human energy is required to prepare earth for building, and there is no pollution produced in the process. Provided nothing bizarre is added to it, earth can be recycled indefinitely. It is fire resistant, capable of absorbing excess humidity, and possesses good thermal properties. Like many local and natural materials, it can be obtained at little or no cost. In contrast, the high price and energy required to manufacture modern industrial materials such as concrete, fired brick, wood frame, and steel has made them unavailable to those most in need. And even if available, building with manufactured materials requires expensive and complicated tools.

Considering the great shortage of humane and comfortable housing around the world, genuine solutions must be based on materials that are local and accessible. Earth is one material that can be considered a viable and realistic option for much of the world.

Hand Coiling or Coursing Wet Earth

While the clay mix is wet and pliable, it can be placed directly on the wall and shaped in place. The clay mix is often shaped into large, snakelike coils or balls, and knitted together once on the wall. After the clay is dry or hard enough, another layer is added. These walls are extremely sculptable and often take on the feel of large pots. Unlike walls that are mortared together like stone or earth blocks, these walls are also more earthquake resistant.

◄ **CÔTE D'IVOIRE. Girl coiling a clay pot uses a common skill of every woman in the village.**

▼ **KAPSIKI, CAMEROON. Hand-formed earth structures.**

◄ **MOULA, CAMEROON.** Mousgoum domes are built without any framework or supports. The protruding ridges add reinforcement to the very thin mud walls. *(below and left)* Interior skylight and ventilation.

◀ **TOGO**. Castle fortresses of the Tamberma people. The walls are built using large balls of earth stacked in layers. The thatched towers are for grain storage. For protection from enemy slave hunters, there is only one entrance into the house, plus two small door-ways into a chicken room. *(left)* Small thatched room on top of the roof for sleeping. It is the place most protected from slave hunters.

MATAM, SENEGAL. The protrusions in the wall help shade openings to improve ventilation via cooler air. The building's exterior is replastered every couple of years with a mixture of cow dung and Senegal River clay.

EGYPT. Making small earthen blocks using a simple wooden form.

Earthen Blocks

EARTHEN BLOCKS ARE crafted in a variety of shapes and sizes. They are the most common earth construction medium used around the world. Blocks are made by packing a wet mud mixture into a form and then immediately removing the form, leaving the mud block on the ground to dry in the sun. Once dry, blocks are mortared in place with mud. The most common mix is a combination of clay and sand with some straw, but a wide variety of additional ingredients are used, depending upon what is locally available. Cow manure is quite common. Traditionally called *adobes* in Spanish and *ottob* in Arabic, earthen blocks can be made by hand or by machine, and production levels range from those made by hand to those churned out by automated factories. Although rectangular blocks are the most common, cylindrical and pyramidical shapes are also found.

Another method of obtaining earthen blocks is cutting them directly from the earth. When the earth contains a high percentage of grass roots, it is called *sod* in the United States and England, *terrone* in Central and South America, and *turf* in some places. Blocks are also cut from hardened soils. They are referred to as *tepetate* in Mexico, *caliche* in the United States, *marl* in England, and *turf* in Mediterranean areas.

▲ **YEMEN. Thin earthen blocks used to build skyscrapers.**

▲ CANELO, ARIZONA. An earth-plastered adobe-block house with porch.

◀ PERU. A Quechua family compound of adobe-block houses.

▲ AMRAN, YEMEN. Elegant stained-glass windows rimmed with lime plaster.

◀ SAADA, YEMEN. Multistoried earthen buildings. Saada is so close to Saudi Arabia, the buildings are influenced by many Arabic traditions. The small overhanging rooms near the top are bathrooms. Because the air is so hot and dry, liquids evaporate before hitting the ground.

▲ **HARRAN, TURKEY.** Conical stone domes covered with earth plaster. The hot air rises to the tops of the domes, keeping the air below cooler.

◄ **SHIBAM, YEMEN.** Skyscrapers more than a thousand years old are made with earthen bricks. The tops of the buildings are painted white with gypsum to reflect heat.

NEAR LAKE TITICACA, PERU. The Quechua Indians live in domes made from earth blocks. The domes have square bases with blocks corbelled to form a conical-shaped roof. *(near left)* Interior of corbelled earth block dome.

Earth **31**

CHIPAYA, BOLIVIA. Near the Chilean border, the elevation is more than 9,834 feet (3,000 meters). The land is quite salty and not much but grass grows. Small conical domes are built from earth blocks dug from the ground.

CHIPAYA, BOLIVIA. Earth blocks dug from the ground.

HIGH PLATEAU, MADAGASCAR. Tall, narrow buildings built from fired earth blocks. The walls are plastered with lime while the roofs are covered with grass.

Compacted Earth

Compacting earth increases its strength and minimizes its vulnerability to water. Varying methods are used around the world to compress or compact earth into thick walls. In the United States this method of earth construction is known as rammed earth. In France, *pisé*, as it is known, has been used for centuries. It has also been used in other European countries, has a history in China, and is still used in Morocco.

On the simplest level, compression can be achieved by tamping the dampened earth into small forms using a mallet or heavy pole. Once well compacted, the form is removed and shifted to an adjacent section of wall, filled with dirt, and again tamped. To mechanize and speed up the process, vibrating compressors and more extensive formwork are employed.

▲ HIGH ATLAS MOUNTAINS, MOROCCO. **Compacting earth in wooden forms.**

◄ RHÔNE ALPS, FRANCE. **Near Grenoble, this three-hundred-year-old rammed-earth house sits on a large stone foundation. Traditionally, rammed earth was common in this area, but now the cost of labor is too expensive for the people to continue this technique.**

▲ MOROCCO. Multistoried rammed-earth buildings. Fortified houses with tall towers are called kasbahs. The original purpose of the towers was for defense.

◄ OSSIKIS VILLAGE, MOROCCO. Rammed-earth towers with stone foundations.

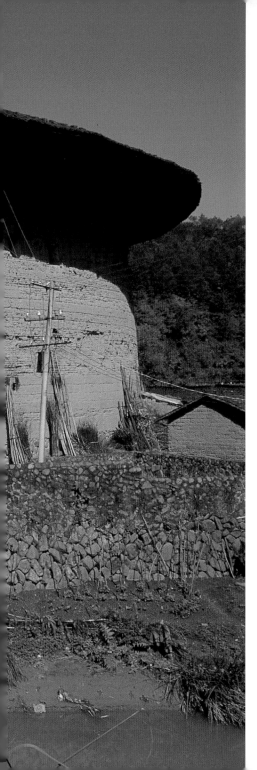

▲ YUNNAN, CHINA. Rammed earth walls with shells because it is very close to a lake and they dig the mud from the lake. A thin strip of white lime plaster on top.

◀ FUJIAN, CHINA. Compact circular family compound. The four-story exterior walls are rammed earth, while the walls within the building's enclosure are built from cedar. The first floor is used for cooking and eating; the second floor is for storage; the third and fourth floors are for sleeping.

Daubed Earth

WHEN EARTH IS infilled into a structural frame, it is referred to as *daub*. It is most commonly inserted into the interstices of a lattice-like work of small poles, reeds, or split bamboo. This is referred to as *wattle and daub*. The earth that is used typically has high clay content and is combined with straw.

However, the same type of mix is also used in conjunction with a variety of other techniques. Thicker walls of earth and fibers are built with structures that have much less extensive latticework. In this case, the wall construction is more one of placing earth balls, or *cob*, into the structure. Putting reels of earth and straw into structures is another variation of the daubed-earth technique.

▲ CHITWAN, NEPAL. Young girl mixing cow dung and clay to be plastered over the reeds.

◄ SUIKHET, NEPAL. Village houses are oval-shaped wattle-and-daub with thatch roofs and large porches. The interior floors are made of compacted earth.

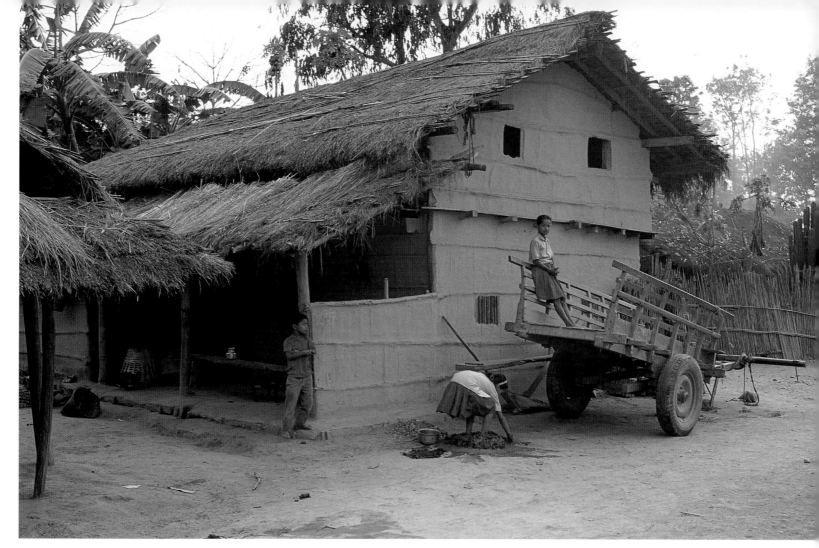

CHITWAN, NEPAL. Clay-based paint colors these Tharu people's wattle-and-daub thatched houses with porches.

VERACRUZ, MEXICO. Wattle and daub for this house is made of long-cut wheat straw mixed with orange earth.

SONORA, MEXICO. Yaqui Indian wattle-and-daub construction using carrizo reed with mesquite posts.

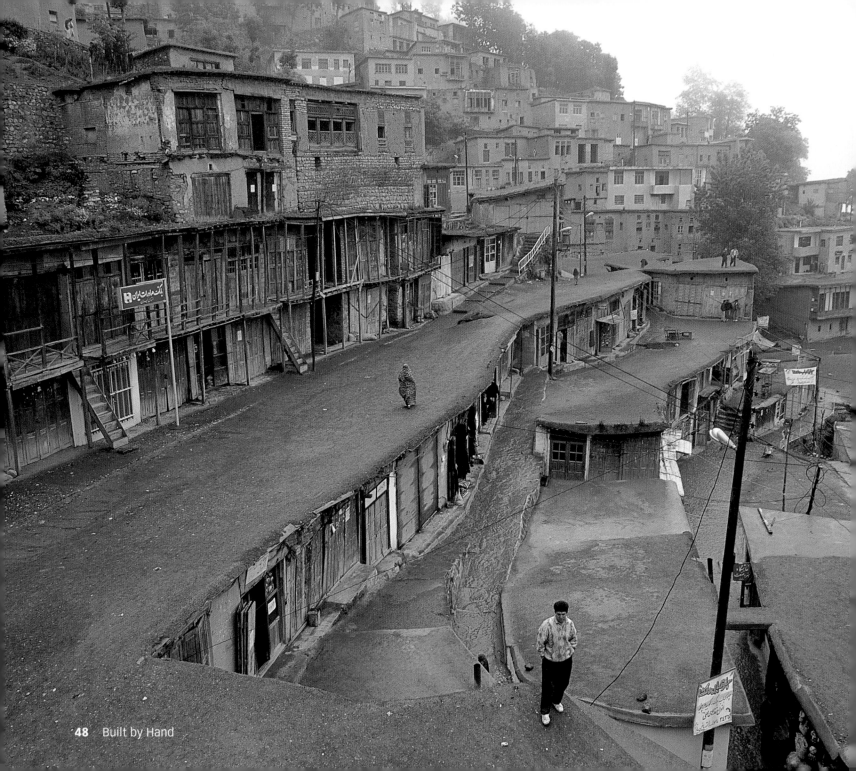

Earthen Roofs

EARTH CAN BE used as a roofing material in a variety of ways. It is most commonly used as a flat roof surface in hot, dry climates. Typically, different types of earth are packed on top of wood poles and branches, but it is also used on top of other structural materials, including metal poles and concrete. Their main disadvantages are that they are extremely heavy and waterproofing is extremely difficult. Special soils and additives are often employed to improve their effectiveness. One of the greatest advantages, however, of flat earthen roofs is their use as extra living space. They can provide additional useful space to be used for food and clothes drying, storage, cooking, and sleeping. Where buildings are clustered closely together, the flat roofs of adjoining buildings are often used as passageways and secondary streets.

The use of earth is not limited to flat roofs. It can also be used as a covering for pitched roofs. Depending upon local resources, numerous approaches have been used, but the majority rely upon techniques that combine clay soils with long fibers. These include shingles and panels as well as wrapping mixtures of clay and straw around sticks to form reels. When fired, clay is used as both tiles and bricks, with clay sometimes being used as a mortar.

When structural timber is in short supply, roofs have been made by forming earth into vaults or cupolas (domes).

▲ HARRAN, TURKEY. Conical stone domes covered with earth plaster.

◄ MASULE, IRAN. These tightly clustered buildings rise up the slope of a hill, with little space between them. The rooftops create multilevel traffic ways.

KASSENA, BURKINA FASO, AFRICA. Accessed by ladders, the earth roofs of these houses are used for storing a variety of items, drying food, sleeping, cooking, and more.

Earth Plaster

IN MANY CLIMATES, earth-built walls hold up to weather and erosion, provided they are built on good foundations and are protected at the top, especially with good roof overhangs. Good design and well-executed techniques can often eliminate the need for plaster, except where there is great need for protection from the elements. However, lack of materials and/or conflicting building traditions may prevent this. In such cases, a special type of coating is required as a defense against the weather. The same shield will usually guard against damage from abrasion as well as improve the aesthetic appearance.

More than any other plaster around the world, earth is used widely on the exterior of earth buildings to provide this type of resistance. However, without the inclusion of additional materials, earth has limited capability as an exterior plaster in that it is susceptible to erosion. Despite this, it is capable of providing needed protection to the walls but must be repaired and maintained on a regular basis. The earth plaster is the layer that is expected to wear—not the walls of the building. Applying a lime wash or paint made from local materials often increases the durability of these plasters.

Earth-based plasters, which can be beautifully colored, lend themselves to a great variety of artistic applications. Sculptural forms and reliefs are easily created as well, and can be finished with clay paints.

▲ TOUCOULEUR, SENEGAL Clay and cow dung.

◄ GUJARAT, INDIA Woman plastering with a mixture of clay and cow dung.

BURKINA FASO, AFRICA. Woman plastering with clay and cow dung.

Stone

IN ITS NATURAL CONTEXT, stone can look breathtaking, as exquisite massive shapes, color and texture come together. Stone masonry work around the world is no less so. The mortarless joints at Machu Picchu in Peru, the multistoried structures of Chaco Canyon in the American Southwest, the carved rock sculptures of ancient India and the Arabic temples at Petra in eastern Africa invoke a sense of wonder and amazement.

On the other hand, simple stonework can be every bit as beautiful. Care and precision produce marvelous results with the most ordinary stones. Whether spectacular or simple, these examples become even more treasured as quality stonework continues to disappear, becoming increasingly invisible in today's world.

By virtue of its weight and durable qualities, stone implies the intent to stay in one place for some time. Clearly it is not the material of nomads or of modern civilization. Stonework is slow and tedious. More time can be spent looking for the right rock than is required to set it in place. Building with stone actually has more in common with puzzle work than construction.

Stonework can be exacting and meticulous or sloppy and irregular. Stones can be laid up mortarless like the parabolic trulli domes, or they can utilize earth-, lime-, or cement-based mortars. Many small pieces can be fit together, or large boulders can be incorporated into walls like those in the hilltop village of Monsanto, Portugal.

Having good strength and impermeability, stone is a durable wall material and is

▲ HOVENWEEP, UTAH.

◄ THE OLGAS IN ABORIGINAL LAND, AUSTRALIA.

especially suitable for foundations and stem walls in combination with other materials such as earth or wood. It is an excellent source of thermal mass for helping maintain stable indoor temperatures, but it is also a very poor insulator. As a roofing material, stone makes excellent shingles. It is widely used for field walls, cobblestone roads, and terraces. And on a larger scale, it has been used to build bridges, roads and fortresses.

Despite the widespread availability of stone, there are a variety of reasons why it has not been used more widely. Some types of stone are better suited for building than others: sizes and shapes vary. Masonry techniques from place to place vary as much as stone does. The tools to trim or carve a particular type of stone may not be available or suitable for shaping. Little definitive how-to information exists about building with stone. Stone also resists standardization, thereby making it difficult to create building codes except when it is combined with the industrial staples of cement and steel reinforcement.

◄ **HIGH ATLAS MOUNTAINS, MOROCCO.** Decorative stonework.

▶ **TOUDJANE, TUNISIA.** Stone buildings and vaulted structures.

CHACO CANYON, NEW MEXICO. Anasazi stone ruins.

▲ WALATA, MAURITANIA. **Men hauling mud to mortar the upper courses of stone.**

◄ MONSANTO, PORTUGAL. **Stone house built over a large rock.**

Stone **63**

▲ TUNISIA. A *ghorfa*, or vaulted storeroom. The stones are mortared and plastered with clay.

◄ NANDO, MALI. Stone complex in Dogon villlage.

◄ **SHIMSHAL VALLEY, PAKISTAN.** Close to the Chinese border, stone houses are built at the base of the mountain. They were previously used as a political prison. *(below)* Each house has a skylight for illumination and ventilation for an otherwise dark and windowless interior.

WUILLOW, PERU. A village of stone houses and houses thatched with grass. The villagers express color and decoration through their clothes and fabrics made from llama wool.

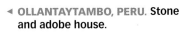

◄ **OLLANTAYTAMBO, PERU.** Stone and adobe house.

▲ OLLANTAYTAMBO, PERU. Old Inca stonework.

▶ CAPPADOCIA, TURKEY. Stone arches extended on to the front of simple dwellings carved into the soft volcanic rock.

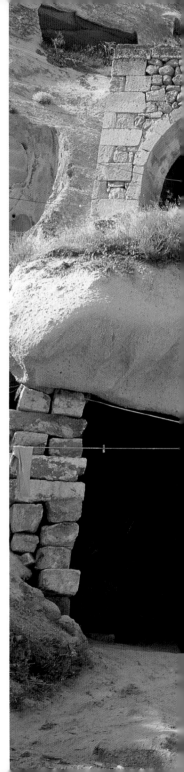

◄ **AL-MUKALLA, YEMEN.** Tiny fortress on a hill.

◄ **AL-HAJJARA, YEMEN.** *(middle)* A fortress village on a hill with multistory stone houses. For defensive reasons there is only one entrance to the village. Window openings are finished with lime.

◄ **JAISALMER, INDIA.** *(far left)* Yellow stone houses. Decorated windows and balconies are carved from the soft stone.

▲ SANTORINI, GREECE. Domed and vaulted stone roofs. Lime wash is used regularly for maintenance.

▶ TINOS, GREECE. Room for washing.

◀ ALBEROBELLO, ITALY. Trulli houses. *Trullo* (singular) comes from the Greek word *truddu*, meaning cupola, and refers to cone-shaped stone roofs built on a rectangular base. The interior of the roof looks like a parabolic dome.

MONSANTO, PORTUGAL. Rock within rock.
Stone houses built beneath and within rocks.

▲ GUERRERO, MEXICO. Stone
slate is used for roofs and
paving.

◀ DHAMPUS, NEPAL. Stone-slate
roofs and stone retaining wall.

PENALBA DE SANTIAGO, GALICIA, SPAIN. In this small, remote mountain village along the Camino de Santiago pilgrimage route, slate roofs and walls are made of unmortared (dry stack) stone. Balconies are a dominant architectural feature in this town where heavy snows cause muddy streets.

► **TRONGSA, BHUTAN.** Stones are placed on the roof to help weigh it down against strong winds.

◄ KINNAUR, INDIA. Nicely detailed wood houses with gray slate roofs in Kalpa.

Limestone as Plaster and Paint

LIME IS USED AS a breathable plaster and paint to both adorn and protect earthen and stone walls from weather and abrasion. Where the climate is extreme or extra strength is required, lime is most frequently applied as a plaster rather than a thin paint. However, careless application and lack of technical know-how can result in problems with lime plaster. Care must be taken in mixing the plaster, preparing the surface where it will be used, and applying it.

In an effort to counter lime's sensitivity, cement has replaced the use of lime in many regions, mostly because it sets quickly and forms a hard surface. However, cement is very inflexible and therefore incompatible with most traditional wall materials. It can also retard the evaporation of moisture in the walls, leading to serious problems later.

Lime is referred to as a wash when it is used as paint. Lime wash provides some degree of protection, although it can easily be washed or dusted off the wall. Nonetheless, it is easy to use and can be reapplied frequently. It can be made more durable with the addition of a wide variety of stabilizers that include oils, glues, salts and plant juices. In addition to providing protection from the weather, lime wash has strong antiseptic qualities.

▲ WEST COAST, IRELAND. Lime-plastering a thatched house.

◄ MATMATA, TUNISIA. Limewashing the walls of an underground courtyard to help reflect light.

Wood

IN ADDITION TO being beautiful, wood is suitable for construction in virtually every climate zone. As trees cover approximately one-third of the earth's landmass, wood is widely used for almost every facet of construction, including the structure, walls, roof, ceiling, doors, windows, shingles, and furniture. It has respectable thermal qualities and is durable.

It is compatible with traditional skills and doesn't require sophisticated equipment or processing. When processed, less energy is needed than for most other materials. At the same time, there are many species and forms suitable for all kinds of applications. This diversity necessitates familiarity and knowledge about the different varieties and their potential uses so they can be used effectively.

Timber can be renewable and sustainable, provided that reforestation is carried out and natural habitats protected. The rapid loss of old-growth forests, the depletion of trees due to uncontrolled cutting, and the environmental degradation that follows deforestation are major concerns associated with wood's use. Understanding and dealing with these issues is critical, as it is not possible to completely replace wood with other materials. It is a fundamental and

▲ KONSO, ETHIOPIA. The Konso people call these carved wood figures that stand at the entrance of the village "ancestors."

◄ SHIMSAL, PAKISTAN.

▲ **NIAS, INDONESIA.** Passageway formed by the joinery at the base of the omo sebua, a house used by the traditional chief. It is one of the world's largest wooden houses.

▶ **BHUTAN.** Sawing a large timber.

basic building material throughout the world and great efforts are needed to insure its longevity for future generations.

Construction timber is divided into primary and secondary classifications. Primary refers to slow-grown hardwoods that inherently have high natural resistance; secondary timbers are fast-grown species of lower durability. Pole timbers that are generally taken from young trees are stronger than sawed wood and save the cost and waste of cutting. Sawed lumber typically comes from larger diameter trunks.

Wherever timber is found, varying construction methods have evolved. Traditional woodbuilding techniques can be fundamentally divided according to whether timber is sawed or used as poles. Throughout much of the world, simple pole structures are common. Bigger poles or logs are laid in a horizontal position to support the weight of the roof. Sawed lumber is used in timber-frame or post-and-beam construction where different types of joinery are employed.

▲ WALATA, MURITANIA.

▲▲ TINOS, GREECE.

Horizontal Log Construction

IN HORIZONTAL APPLICATION, the mass and dead weight of the poles or logs support all the vertical loads, unlike structures where the weight from above is transferred to vertical posts through horizontal beams. Sometimes the logs are whole; at other locations they are sawed into thick, broad planks or split lengthwise. When split or sawed, a tighter joint results.

◄ CANYON DE CHELLY, ARIZONA. Navajo hogan. The roof structure is built using horizontally laid logs in an overlapping hexagonal pattern that is covered with dirt.

► SHIP ROCK, NEW MEXICO. Modern Navajo hogan where the logs are covered with local soil. The woman is weaving a rug on the giant loom.

▲ **KINNAUR, INDIA**. Horizontal logs with earth fill.

◄ **WYOMING**. Log cabin at the base of the Rocky Mountains.

VLKOLINEC, SLOVAKIA. Log houses in the "Village Hidden by God" that is also known as the "Wolf's Village." They are painted inside and out with colored lime wash. The hip roofs are covered with wood shingles. Traditionally, a figure or adornment is carved into the wood near the peak. Bells are used as an alarm signal.

▲ SWISS ALPS, SWITZERLAND. Oak and pinewood houses near Zermatt.

◄ CICMANY, SLOVAKIA. Geometric patterns painted with lime wash. The photographer first visited this village in the early 1970s; when he returned thirty years later, life in the village and the style of building remained unchanged.

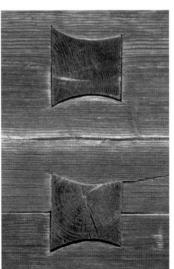
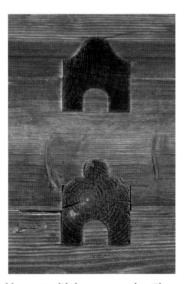

ALPBACH, AUSTRIA. Tirol-style wood houses with large verandas. The large lower-level space is used for cows.

CHINA. Timber-frame construction.

Frameworks of Wood

THE SIMPLEST WOOD framework system uses small and unprocessed poles, forked at the top and anchored in the ground for stability. A beam is laid across the forked poles, and the roof structure is connected to it. The structural components are typically lashed together. The basic techniques are essentially the same all over the world.

When bigger timbers are used with large buildings, they are often squared and trimmed, relying upon joinery instead of lashing. The terms *timber frame* and *post-and-beam construction* are used in conjunction with these types of frameworks, although in a modern context, post-and-beam can mean something very different. Current-day post-and-beam structures often rely upon manufactured metal plates instead of joinery to make connections. In traditional buildings the joints are sometimes halved; in others, tenon joints are used. But with both methods, the timbers are normally secured with wooden pegs. Diagonal bracing is accomplished by using a lot of small wood members—curved braces and the like.

The frame is essentially a stand-alone structure that requires infill material between the upright posts. The most common method may have been mixtures of straw and clay in combination with wattles of branches. However, infills of stone, fired brick, and earth blocks have been used. Depending upon the infill material, the walls may or may not be plastered with earth or lime, or covered with claddings of wood, stone, or brick. In many, the upper floors extend beyond the level below to provide weather protection and good drainage for water that contacts the upper part of the building.

TRANSYLVANIA, ROMANIA. Basic timber-frame construction and wood shingles.

YUCATÁN, MEXICO. Typical Mayan dwelling with thatched hip roof and structure of small poles lashed together.

◄ **YUCATÁN, MEXICO.** A detail unique to the pole structures of Yucatán is that the end walls are curved to form an apse. Instead of horizontal latticework, the walls are finished with vertical poles, or *cololches,* that are packed with leaves and branches and daubed with earth. *(above)* The Yucatán is known for its hammocks. They easily transform a living space into a sleeping area. They provide good ventilation, keeping one off the ground and away from insects and pests.

NORTHERN NIAS, INDONESIA. Large family compound. On this island there are many of these large, circular pole structures, one for each extended family. Along the outer edge is a community space with built-in benches, similar to seating on a bus or ship. Diagonals are added to the vertical posts to provide horizontal reinforcement for earthquakes that are frequent on this island. *(above)* Wood joint.

▲ **KINNAUR, INDIA.** Large timber-frame structure with wood panels for infill in this Rakcham village.

◄ **SULAWESI, INDONESIA.** The Torajas people use wood for the building structure of their traditional tongkonan houses. Bamboo is used for other parts of the house, including the shingles.

▲ YAMAGATA PREFECTURE, JAPAN. This five-story pagoda, or tiered tower, in Mount Haguro-san dates to the fourteenth century. Japanese cedar (Cryptomeria japonica) surrounds it.

► THIMPHU, BHUTAN. Trashi Chhoe Dzong, an ornately decorated temple. The timber frame has wood infill.

◄ **SAFRANBOLU, TURKEY.** Timber-frame house with block and stone infill. The upper stories cantilever over the lower floors, providing protection from the weather.

▲ **CASTLE COMBE, ENGLAND.**

Color and Cladding

WOOD BUILDINGS ARE often clad with overlapping wood shingles, shakes, or siding. Like the feathers of a bird, they are very effective at shedding water. Shingles are cut and shaped with a saw; shakes are hand-split. Whereas roof shingles and shakes are often plain and without color, shingles used to cover walls are commonly colored or cut into a variety of interesting shapes to form decorative patterns.

CHILOE ISLAND, CHILE.

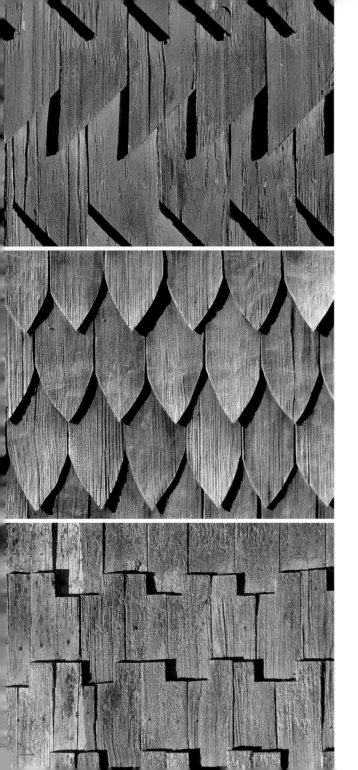

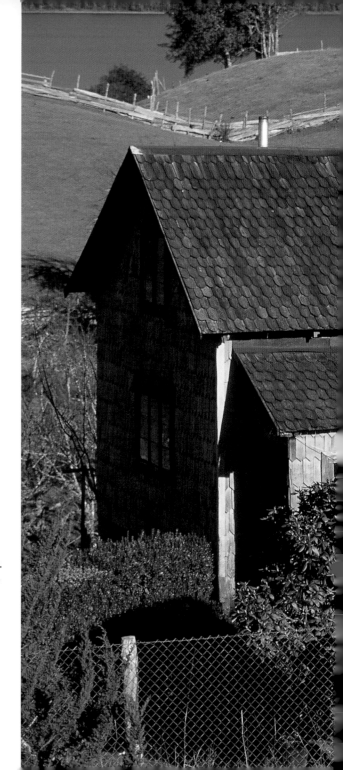

CHILOE ISLAND, NEAR PUERTO MONTT, CHILE. In the southern part of Chile, where wood is plentiful, all houses are built from wood and covered with ornate wood shingles. Shingles, or *tejulas*—long, thin, narrow pieces of alerce wood. They are used for covering both roofs and walls. *(left)* All three are detail examples of this style of wood.

GOLDEN RING, RUSSIA. "Golden Ring" refers to an area in the north-eastern part of Moscow where shelters are built in the Old Russian style.

MEIRINGEN, SWITZERLAND. The use of highly detailed wood shingles is declining, as the material is expensive and the application is labor intensive. Small fish-scale-like shingles cover the brown house.

MARAMURES, ROMANIA. Wood timber houses with wood roof shingles. The small, eye-shaped openings in the roof provide ventilation. The house has two rooms connected by a kitchen in the middle.

◄ MARAMURES, ROMANIA. Wood timber houses with wood roof shingles.

▲ ANGAHUAN, MICHOACAN, MEXICO. In this Purepecha village, the houses are built primarily of wood, including the roof shingles.

LOFOTEN ISLAND, NORWAY.
Wood houses with "living" sod roofs. The roofs are covered with soil and grass, improving insulation for these homes located in the Arctic Circle zone.

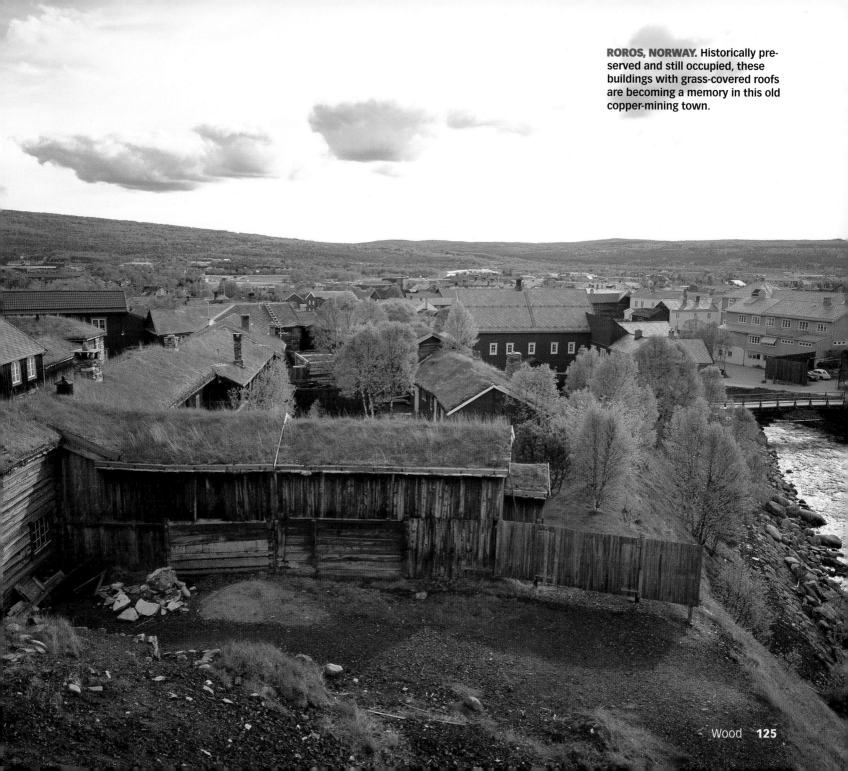

ROROS, NORWAY. Historically preserved and still occupied, these buildings with grass-covered roofs are becoming a memory in this old copper-mining town.

Bamboo, Grasses, and Other Plants

THE GRASS FAMILY has served as one of the major building materials for traditional cultures, especially in warmer climates where entire buildings may be built from it. In many areas it is found in great profusion, proliferating where other plant materials, such as trees, are in short supply.

Bamboo is the largest member of the grass family, with some 1,200 species scattered throughout the world. Some attain heights of more than ninety feet with culms that are six inches in diameter. Basically there are two types: clumping varieties that are common to warmer regions, and running bamboo that is found in more temperate regions. Its rate of growth is incredible, needing just three to five years to achieve a level of strength that is suitable for construction. On a similar-size piece of land, its annual yield can be twenty-five times more than the yield of forests. Small plots can provide enough to supply a family with all that is needed for building and a variety of other uses.

Reeds are long-stemmed, water- or marsh-growing grasses that lack the structural strength of bamboo. Nevertheless, reeds are flexible and elastic and can be easily woven. They are capable of playing a major role in construction, especially when used in combination with other materials. Some of the most famous reed buildings are constructed by the Ma'dan people who inhabit the marshes between the confluence of the Tigris and Euphrates Rivers in Iraq. They bundle twenty-foot lengths of phragmites, or *qasab,* as it is known to them, to build incredible arched structures

▲ EAST COAST, MADAGASCAR.
Working with bamboo.

◄ FLORES, INDONESIA. **Bamboo.**

that exhibit some of the most ingenious skills utilized in areas with scarce resources.

Common grasses and straw are used in both hot and cold climates as roofing material to provide thick, insulating cover. However, straw is used less frequently, as the modern and shorter varieties are not as durable or useful as heirloom varieties.

The leaves of larger trees, such as the palm and banana, also play vital roles as building materials and are often used in conjunction with members of the grass family. In certain parts of Mexico, the leaves of the agave cactus, or century plant, are used for constructing the walls and roofs of dwellings. Other parts of the cactus family are also used for building, especially the ribs or skeletons of the larger species such as the organ pipe and saguaro that are used as part of roof structures, walls, and fences.

SAN BLAS, PANAMA.
Palm houses on the edge
of the ocean.

Bamboo

The uses to which bamboo poles (culms) are put is virtually endless. Common uses include posts, beams, roof and wall structures, stairs, ladders, scaffolding, bridge construction, pipes, fencing, furniture and musical instruments. The high tensile strength of bamboo's weight ratio makes it an ideal structural material. Split culms make excellent purlins, roof tiles, gutters, doors, windows, flooring, plywood, reinforcement for concrete and wall panels. Other uses include fishing poles, bowls, baskets, mats, woven panels and ornamental screens. For many the shoots are a staple food.

▲ TAKAYAMA, JAPAN. Split bamboo used as a screen to protect the bottom of the walls from rain and snow.

◄ FLORES, INDONESIA. *(far left)* The porches of traditional houses in Ngada villages are made from bamboo that is split and laid like overlapping tiles.

◄ BAN NANGANG, LAOS. Flattened bamboo used for the roof. *(above)* Exterior of the roof. *(below)* Interior of the roof.

CHENCHA, ETHIOPIA. Walls made from split bamboo. *(above)* Pots made from split bamboo and covered with cow dung and soil to seal them.

BAN SONG CHA, LAOS. Life in this Mhong village revolves around bamboo. *(above)* A Mhong woman making bamboo paper. *(right)* Bamboo floating in water.

▲ BAN NANGANG, LAOS. This Lue village uses bamboo for every part of the house. The structure is built from wood poles, while flattened bamboo is used for the roof and woven for the walls and floor mats.

◄ MYANMAR Bamboo houses near Inle Lake. The structure is a mix of bamboo poles and wood. The walls are of woven bamboo.

FLORES, INDONESIA. Walls of woven bamboo in Wolowaru village. The house is thatched with alang-alang grass and the walls are painted with patterns of human figures. *(inset)* Interior with earth floor and bamboo-mat ceiling in Lombok Island.

SUMBA, INDONESIA. Four main posts provide the structural support in this building, and bamboo is used for everything else. Symbolically, the tall section of the roof is for God, the middle space for man, and the ground level for animals.

▲ **SULAWESI, INDONESIA.** The Toradja's traditional *tongkonan* houses. Curiously the
houses are built in the shape of a ship
even though they are located in the
mountains. It is speculated that the Torad-
jas' ancestors arrived by boat. The houses
are very large, yet the actual living space
beneath the roof is small. Being so tall,
the roofs offer minimal shade and little
protection from rain. Split bamboo is used
for the roof tiles.

▶ **SUMATRA, INDONESIA.** Thatched Batak
houses in Lingga village on the Karo
plateau. Each house accommodates one
extended family. The upper gable ends are
ornately adorned with woven bamboo
designs and the gable ends of the roof
with buffalo heads.

CHENCHA, ETHIOPIA. These Dorze people's basket houses are made from bamboo poles covered with the leaves of ensete, a type of banana. Split bamboo is woven through the bamboo poles to form the walls. The entrances are covered with hoods, or "noses," which serve as extra protection from the elements.

CHENCHA, ETHIOPIA. In addition to the roofs of houses, the ensete root makes a starch that the Ethiopians store in the ground until it ferments and then either make bread or a beverage from it. Shirts, as well, are made from the same plant. This Dorze village is also known for its high-quality woven cotton cloth. *(left)* Ensete leaves stapled with bamboo. *(upper)* Grating an ensete root. *(right)* Woven bamboo wall.

SAN BLAS, PANAMA. In the Gulf of Mexico, 365 islands line the mainland. The islands are surrounded by coconut palms. On these islands the Cuna Indians use a combination of bamboo, reed, and palm leaves to build.

Reeds and Canes

ETHIOPIA

ZEBILA, GHANA. Millet canes, Kusasi people's compound.

LAKE TITICACA, PERU. The lives of the Aymara or Uros Indians who live at 13,000 feet above sea level revolve around the totora reeds, which provides them with their land, homes, transportation, and food. In the shallow areas of the lake, they mound reed and earth on top of existing reeds to form immense floating islands. The roots of the reeds keep the islands from drifting. The natives navigate the lake on canoes made from tapered bundles of reeds that are bound together with grass ropes, and the reeds serve as walls and floors as well.

NORTHERN THAILAND. Refugee farmhouses near Mae Sai are made from bamboo and wood. Roofs are thatched with palm and grass. There are cross figures on the ridge of the roof.

ETHIOPIA.
Gurage people's houses combine reeds with wattle-and-daub walls.

157

OUVEA, NEW CALEDONIA. Thatched houses with palm walls. The island is covered with coral, and since coral is actually a soft surface, the interior floors are left in that same medium.

House built from the traveler's tree. Walls are made from the skin of the stalk and the roofs from the leaves.

SOUTHERN NIAS, INDONESIA. Palm roofs with
large hinged windows in the roof. *(left)* Palm leaves
for roof.

NEAR PUCALLPA, PERU. Palm leaves used to thatch the walls and the roof.

165

SEPIC RIVER, PAPUA NEW GUINEA. The Sago palm is extremely important to the Papua New Guinea communities. It is not only their main building material but also one of their main food staples. Posts are made from the trunk of the palm, wall shingles and the roof from the leaves, and floors from the skin of the trunk. Sago-palm pound cakes are made from the starch produced by soaking the cut palm trunk in water. The Tambanum village's house is similar to their spiritual house, called haus tambaran. *(See page 381.)*

Bamboo, Grasses, and Other Plants   **167**

CARIBBEAN COAST, COLOMBIA.
A hut of the Guajiro (or Wayuu) people, made from cactus ribs, on the Guajira Peninsula.

HIDALGO, MEXICO. Agave (century plant) leaves are used for the roof and walls.

Thatch

THATCH IS THE world's most common roofing material. It is claimed that India alone has more than forty million thatched buildings. A wide variety of vegetable materials are used, including grasses, reeds, leaves, and tree bark. Thatching materials are renewable resources that typically come from naturally occurring local vegetation, the by-products of food or cash crop agriculture, or through the cultivation of a plant grown specifically for thatching. Water reed *(Phragmites communis)* is considered by most to be the best thatching material. But in general, stiff stem grasses and reeds, three to six feet (one to two meters) in height and up to three-eighths inch (ten millimeters) in diameter at the cut end, are satisfactory.

Straw from cereal grains, mostly wheat and rye, are used for thatch. Preferably both straw and reeds need to be hollow-stemmed and straight to facilitate drying. Palm and other leaves are typically used in tropical areas. Whatever the source, it is important that the thatching material is grown without the addition of nitrogen fertilizers, otherwise it is prone to early decay.

Thatch is labor intensive, which means that in the developed world it will be very expensive. But in areas where time and efficiency aren't driving forces, it can be inexpensive, as there is little or no cost for the material. Thatched roofs are efficient: they provide a roof surface to protect against the weather, they effectively insulate against extremes of temperature, and they make decorative ceilings. In some buildings the walls as well as the roofs are thatched.

▲ CÔTE D'IVOIRE. **Preparing for the cone of the roof.**

◄ KYOTO PREFECTURE, JAPAN. **Reed-and-grass thatching.**

A good-quality roof can be up to twelve inches (thirty centimeters) thick and has a preferred angle of forty-five degrees. The ridge is the most vulnerable part of the roof and is finished differently, depending upon the material used for the thatch and the availability of other materials.

The ridge cap needs to be carefully detailed to make it water resistant, but other weather-resistant materials such as clay tiles and live plants are also used in combination with the main thatching material. High-quality workmanship can produce a roof that has a life expectancy of twenty-five to seventy-five years. Many of the simple and traditional types of thatch have shorter durability.

Probably the major drawback of thatch roofs is their combustibility, but good-quality workmanship and commonsense precautions can reduce that risk significantly. Their functionality and beauty easily warrant their widespread use. There is nothing comparable to entering a shelter with one of these roofs and feeling the drastic difference in temperature. Like a thick blanket, thatch is effective at keeping the heat in or out. And unlike most other roofing materials, it is permeable and able to "breathe."

▶ **NGAOUNDÉRÉ, CAMEROON.**

▶ ▶ **NABUSIMAKE, COLOMBIA.**

▲ **CHITWAN, NEPAL.** Grass thatch.

◀ **HUNGARY.** Water-reed thatch.

◀◀ **OUVEA, NEW CALEDONIA.** Palm and grass thatch.

▲ **AMAZONAS, VENEZUELA.** This village of the Piaroa indigenous people is located near Puerto Ayacucho. Close to the river, the village is accessed only by boat. These circular huts, called *churuatas,* are thatched with palm and occupied by families with as many as twenty members.

◄ **ETHIOPIA.** Grass-thatched huts. Many ethnic groups live around Lake Abaya.

LIFU, NEW CALEDONIA. Melanesian-style round sleeping huts, thatched with palm and grass. When those living on this island marry, they are only permitted to build an *uma ne mekol,* which means "where to sleep." These traditional houses are different from those on the mainland, where everything is modern French style. *(below)* The fireplace has a fire all the time, even in summer.

▲ **NIOFOIN, CÔTE D'IVOIRE.** In this Senoufo village the buildings used for spiritual purposes have tall, pointed thatch roofs that make them higher than other dwellings. The bulbous entrance is also unique to this spiritual house.

◀ **NGAOUNDÉRÉ, CAMEROON.** Head chief's house, or "Lamido's palace," where houses are mosques. The Hausa people call this housing style *saré*.

Thatch **183**

TITHAMAH, YEMEN. Near the Red Sea, a hut is uniquely thatched with tihami reed, which is tied down by doum palm rope to guard against frequent severe storms. The walls are built of earth with reed cladding.

KONSO, ETHIOPIA. Mushroom-shaped thatch buildings, built very close to one another. Clay pots on top keep the peak of the roof from leaking. *(right)* Interior of thatched ceiling.

▲ TLAXCALA, MEXICO. Walls and roof of rye thatch in El Carmen Tequexquitla. A group of several structures make up the house—the cooking room, sleeping room, granary, and steam bathroom.

◄ LUZON, PHILIPPINES. The Ifugao people converted old rice granaries into dwellings. The living quarters are contained within the pyramidal thatch roofs. During World War II, when the Japanese army marched through the area, these people disassembled their houses, covered them with dirt, and escaped to the mountains until the army left.

CASAMANCE, SENEGAL. Due to the unavailability of anything but salinated water, this Eloubaline village by the sea uses inverted thatched roofs for collecting rainwater. Each family complex has one.

The central opening (left) also provides light to the circular interior of these "impluvium" dwellings.

▲ NATAL, SOUTH AFRICA. Zulu round houses with conical thatched roofs.

► GUJARAT, INDIA. Grass-thatched conical roofs in this Ludia village are secured by rope to counteract the strong ocean winds. The walls are built of earth, covered with a mix of clay and cow dung, and then painted with decorative designs. Clay tiles are becoming common as grass becomes increasingly difficult to find.

FLORES, INDONESIA. Ngada people's houses in Bena village have totems and megaliths set into the plazas. The female totem (right front) is a thatched house-like shrine that is open on one side. The male totem is a pole three meters (ten feet) high with umbrella thatch (left front). *(above)* Carved wooden panel in the inner sanctuary of a Ngada ancestral home.

▲ **YUNNAN PROVINCE, CHINA.** The region of Xishuangbanna is in the deep south of Yunnan Province near Laos. Called Hani or Akha houses, they have animal storage to the side and are thatched with grass.

◄ **A VILLAGE NEAR OLLANTAYTANBO, PERU.** Thatched earth-block houses in the Andes hillside.

▲ IWATE PREFECTURE, JAPAN.

► GUNMA PREFECTURE, JAPAN. A kotatsu—low table with a heating system—and tatami, or woven reed mats, for sitting.

▲ **KYOTO PREFECTURE, JAPAN.** Traditional farm-houses in Miyama City, thatched with grass and reed. This style of building is rapidly disappearing from modern Japan.

◄ **FUKUSHIMA PREFECTURE, JAPAN.** Traditional Magariya-style house in Mizuhiki village.

PLAINS OF HUNGARY.
Farmhouse thatched with water reed and plastered with lime. Water reeds are plentiful in the grand plain, Puszta, which spreads out around the Duna and Tisza Rivers. *(right)* The domed oven heats both the kitchen and bedroom.

WEST COAST, IRELAND. Lime-plastered house with reed thatch tied down with net and rope. The net is weighted down with stones. Buildings were kept small to counteract the heavy taxes levied by the English when Ireland was a colony. *(above)* Fireplace for heating and cooking. Peat is free, so it is used for fuel.

▲ BRETAGNE, FRANCE. Thatched stone houses in Karascoet.

▶ NORMANDIE, FRANCE. Thatched, timber-frame house with ridge cap of irises.

LÆSO ISLAND, DENMARK. A six-and-a-half-foot (two meters)-thick seaweed thatch over lime-plastered walls. The wood in many buildings is salvaged from shipwrecks.

Drying seaweed for roof.

Detail of seaweed roof from the inside.

LÆSO ISLAND, DENMARK. Seaweed-roofed house.

JAPAN.

INDONESIA.

INISHEER ISLANDS, IRELAND.

MEXICO.

JAPAN.

JAPAN.

Materials
Combined

SOME BUILDINGS cannot be described as having been built with one dominant material. In fact, they are essentially conglomerations of several different materials. Some demonstrate the use of earth, stone, wood, and thatch in relatively balanced proportions, while others may use as few as two material elements.

Materials can be combined when there is a shortage of one and another is needed to finish the project. However, materials can often complement one another, thereby improving their performance. Each has strengths and weaknesses. Stone can be very strong and impermeable to water, making a great foundation material, but it is heavy and insulates poorly. Earth is easy to obtain, requiring little in the way of processing. It makes very comfortable and moldable walls but lacks resistance to water. Wood allows structural flexibility and has longevity, but in arid regions it is also prone to rot, termites, and fire. Its availability is often limited.

In addition to creating a more functional and durable building, combining different materials can also produce beautiful results. Changes in shapes, colors, textures, and patterns can be pleasing to the eye. Using the same material that has been finished in different ways is often striking. Traditionally, the Japanese were masters of combining highly finished materials with rustic ones.

Although unintentional, the seemingly haphazard combination of materials can result in beauty that contrasts to the boring and repetitive nature of modern buildings.

◄▲ **KALASH VALLEY, PAKISTAN. Mortared stone in combination with horizontal wood logs.**

◄◄ **PARO, BHUTAN.** A beautiful combination of wood frame with rammed-earth walls and stone foundation. Male sex organs (phallus) are symbolic of riches or prosperity.

KALASH VALLEY, PAKISTAN. Near the Afghanistan border, the Kalash people use alternating layers of horizontal logs and stone. The flat roofs provide functional space. Unlike their neighbors, the Kalash people have very blue eyes, and many believe they are descendants of Alexander the Great.

◄◄ **OLD MANALI, INDIA.** Located in the Indian Himalaya, a combination of log, stone and earth is used on this dwelling. The cantilevered upper story is for living space while the lower level is for storage and animals.

◄ **NEAR MANALI, INDIA.** The kitchen is located in a loft within the upper part of the roof. It has an earthen floor and a ceiling decoratively plastered with clay.

Materials Combined   **219**

LIJIANG, CHINA. A mix of stone, earth blocks, fired brick, masonry block, and clay roof tiles.

▲ **NEAR LIJIANG, CHINA.** Earth-brick wall on a stone foundation with tiled roof.

◄ **NABUSIMAKE, COLUMBIA.** An Arhuaco Indian house. The foundation is stone, the walls are daubed earth, and the roof is thatched with grass.

FADIOUT, SENEGAL. There are 6,000 people on Shell Island, a mix of Christians and Muslims. In times past, the houses on this island were made of straw, but they burned down. Rather than continue this tradition, houses are now built out of blocks made from sea shells.

Into the Earth

CLIMATE AND SOIL ALLOWING, humans have created habitable space by digging into the earth both horizontally and vertically, often by taking advantage of natural and existing openings. No other structural material is required other than the earth and its own self-supporting properties. Reducing or eliminating the need for manufactured materials dramatically reduces both expense and complexity.

This type of construction is most easily undertaken in soft soils or rock in hot and dry climates. Numerous examples of this type of construction can be found wherever these conditions are prevalent, including the region from southern Europe to northern Africa as well as the Four Corners area of the southwestern United States.

Excavated dwellings provide comfort from extreme temperatures by taking advantage of the earth's mass. They offer protection from prevailing winds and are often well hidden or shielded from enemies. In temperate climates, south-facing cliffs and the sides of hills are more desirable, especially when it becomes possible to build under the protection of an overhanging south-facing cliff to take advantage of solar gain.

The interior of excavated dwellings is often very sculptural; curves and arches are prominent, with little sense of rigid geometry. These spaces can be quite complex, some even having multiple stories. Floor plans are somewhat predictable, with the living and kitchen areas to the front illuminated by the opening and sleeping areas to the rear. Walls and ceilings are typically painted with lime wash to reflect the little light that is available.

▲ KANDVAN, IRAN. Occupied caves in sandstone.

◄ CAPPADOCIA, TURKEY. Dwellings carved into the soft stone.

Where many dwellings are excavated into the earth, such as Matmata in Tunisia, the landscape has a lunarlike appearance due to the numerous crater-size holes in the ground. The holes mark the locations of courtyards that are surrounded by underground rooms. These courtyard spaces allow for easier ventilation to more rooms, as well as better distribution of light.

Groupings such as these can be quite large, requiring sophisticated planning and layout—which is no different from towns aboveground that have businesses, schools, and offices. In China, dugout dwellings have been systematically planned to include thousands of homes and workshops, industries, schools, offices, and hotels laid out on a grid pattern. Some have large central patios that are several hundred meters square, with occupied spaces developed around them that are ventilated by the patios.

Villagelike groupings often develop where a series of caves are found or where the vertical face of an exposed cliff allows easy excavation.

KANDVAN, IRAN (NEAR TABRIZ).
Houses carved into and built at
the base of sandstone cliffs.

CAPPADOCIA, TURKEY. Houses carved out of soft volcanic rock. These caves are still occupied, but to a lesser extent. Bringing water daily from the wells below is very hard work for the women. *(left)* Christian monks lived and received their training in these caves during the third and fourth centuries A.D.

GUADIX, SPAIN. More than 9,000 people—primarily gypsies—occupy cave houses in this area of the Andalusia region.

GUADIX, SPAIN. At the base of the Sierra Nevada, these cave houses are built into hills of earth. The towers are chimneys for ventilation.

COPPER CANYON, MEXICO. The Tarahumara Indians use stone walls to enclose their cave dwellings.

▲ SETENIL, SPAIN. Houses protected under the overhang of the cliff.

▶ MESA VERDE, COLORADO. It was common for the Anasazi Indians to build into cliff openings, which gave their structures protection from the rain, wind, and sun. Often the cliffs faced to the south, allowing the winter sun to enter, but not in summer.

MATMATA, TUNISIA. Underground houses in North Africa by the Mediterranean Sea. These man-made houses carved into the earth appear as moon craters from above. They were originally excavated as hiding places from the Romans and Arabs. The interior rooms of these underground houses are often vaulted. Everything from walls, ceilings, and floors are lime-washed to keep them as light as possible.

UTAH, UNITED STATES. Caves
that have been recently
enclosed.

COOBER PEDY, AUSTRALIA. An opal-mining town of underground caverns. A large drill searching for opals originally makes these caves. When no longer in use, the caves are inhabited by people hoping to strike it rich. Every year someone becomes a millionaire. There are only chimneys—no windows—for ventilation.

COOBER PEDY, AUSTRALIA.

On the Water

OCEANS, RIVERS, AND LAKES are the lifeblood of their surrounding areas. Village existence is closely tied to the abundant resources they offer, including the many varieties of fish, plants, seaweed, and animals. The water is life—a source of food, transportation, commerce, pleasure, and refuge from enemies and fire.

By necessity or for pleasure, some villagers live on the water while others occupy its edge. Where there are protected bays, lakes, navigable rivers, marshes, or areas where water rises and recedes, people have utilized a wealth of strategies to provide shelter for themselves.

Where water levels fluctuate according to seasonal changes, houses are usually built on elevated platforms supported by poles. This is the world of lightweight woven walls and thatch—bamboo, palm, mangrove, and wood poles. Some houses allow fishing directly through the floor.

Others are designed like rafts so that if or when water levels rise, the houses simply float. Some are designed to be permanently in the water, such as small boats that are beautifully and ingeniously crafted to be mobile and to house individual families—whether for a short time or on a permanent basis. Larger upscale and trendy houseboats dot the shorelines of more developed countries.

Where rivers serve as major arteries of communication and travel, clusters of boats often reach the size of dynamic floating cities, complete with traffic lanes and businesses.

▲ NIGER RIVER, MALI.

◄ SULAWESI, INDONESIA.
Drying seaweed.

In some instances, plots of floating land are developed where it is possible to grow vegetables. These plots are bought and sold like real estate. Historically, the Chinese used large timber bamboo to construct rafts the size of small islands. These floating structures reached the size of small villages with nearly two hundred families living upon them, complete with animals, gardens, and orchards.

History is full of examples of floating vessels that included fortresses and churches. The most famous of all is probably Noah's ark. In a modern context, some shipping and military vessels can reach the proportions of a small town.

▶ BOUBON, NIGER. Water signifies life, and many daily activities revolve around the Niger River's edge.

TONLE SAP LAKE, CAMBODIA. Houses on stilts near and on the lake. The Mekong River floods during the rainy season and runs uphill to a lake that swells to five times its dry-season size. Large, hinged shutters keep out the rain.

INLE LAKE, MYANMAR. Intha people's bamboo-and-palm houses on stilts. Small floating islands are sold and traded as plots for growing vegetables.

◀ LAKE NOKWÉ, BENIN. The families
of fishermen live on the lake primarily
for security. Canoes are the main
transportation.

▲ SEPIK RIVER, PAPUA NEW GUINEA. Houses built
of sago palms on the edge of the Sepic River,
which is the main thoroughfare for the region.

PUCALLPA, PERU. The upper Amazon River during the rainy season. The houses float on large balsa-wood logs, which are quite light.

ORINOCO DELTA, VENEZUELA.
The houses of the Warao Indians
are built without walls as the mild
climate makes them unnecessary.

◄▲ **SULAWESI, INDONESIA.** On the ocean's edge, houses of the Baju people are built from mangrove and the roofs are thatched with palm. These people grow and sell seaweed for their livelihood.

▲ CHÂU ĐỐC, VIETNAM. Houses built on the water and mobile houseboats inhabit the Mekong Delta.

◄ LANGA LAKE, VIETNAM. The people who live in these floating houses keep fish and alligators to sell.

◄▲ **NIGER RIVER, MALI.** Boats on the Niger River. The river is unique in that it starts very close to the Atlantic Ocean, only five hundred miles away, and heads inland toward the desert. Fishermen who sell their fish to people near Mopti. The covers are a combination of woven grass mats on the outside and rice straw on the inside.

LOFOTEN ISLANDS, NORWAY.
Glacier-carved peaks with fishing
villages on the sea's edge.

Shelter
that Moves

DIFFERENT FORMS of moveable shelter evolved as human beings sought ways to inhabit areas characterized by little rainfall, scant vegetation, and climatic extremes—places where permanent settlement was not possible. By necessity there was a need to move camp frequently as the resource base of game animals, useful plants, or grazing material were depleted. The shelters built around this lifestyle needed to be light and portable as well as easy to assemble and disassemble. Portable structures became larger and more durable with the availability of livestock such as horses and camels that were capable of transporting the structure.

The simplest structures were typically found in areas where little more existed than a random assortment of branches and grasses gathered on-site and covered by mats or skins. As the length of stay in a given place increased, so did the complexity of the structures that evolved. Poles became larger, often peeled, and transported between sites.

The covering for the shelter depended on available materials and climatic conditions. For example, mats provide better ventilation and air movement, while skins are more effective at keeping out the rain. The elegant and simple tepees of the American Plains Indians rely upon animal skin as a cover. Poles are inclined towards the center to form a conical shape and then covered with buffalo hide.

Woven coverings from animal hair, such as goat or yak in colder climates, are also used. The classic example is the black Berber tent found from Mauritania in

▲ MADAGASCAR. **Vaulted room on wheels pulled by water buffalo.**

◄ NEAR DAMBAM VILLAGE, BURKINA FASO, AFRICA. **Woven mat hut**.

Morocco to Tibet in the East. The dark color of the tent creates dense shade and insulates against the heat. The open weave permits the circulation of air and contracts tightly to keep out rain.

Another class of woven tents includes those that use a cover of thick wool felt in combination with a complicated structure of wood lattice and poles in compression via a rope that wraps round the structure and a compression ring at the top. No posts or pillars are used. The classic example, found throughout central Asia, is commonly known as a yurt, or *ger*, as it is called in Mongolia. When ventilation is needed, the sides can be rolled up. Additional layers of felt may be added when more insulation is required.

The human urge to be on the move lives on today in the outdoor camping tent. Tents are equipped with fiberglass poles and nylon coverings, and are more lightweight than ever. With the arrival of petroleum- and consumer-based lifestyles came a class of moveable shelter tied to motorized transport. Flatbed and pickup trucks were fitted with custom campers. School buses were customized mobile living quarters as they became the precursors to the modern-day recreational vehicle. Pull-behind trailers were developed for those wanting to separate their vehicles from their living quarters.

◀▶ NEAR DAMBAM VILLAGE, BURKINA FASO, AFRICA. The Fulani people who live near the Niger border make huts by using small poles and woven mats. Farmers hire these nomadic people to watch their cows and collect the dung for use in the fields. The high dome shape helps keep the living area cool.

MOROCCO. The common "black tent" that is found throughout the Mideast and Africa. The Berber people in this photo use them when watching sheep during the winter. They are made from goat hair that is woven relatively loosely to allow ventilation; yet it contracts tightly when wet to keep out the rain. The dark color of the tent creates dense shade and insulates against the heat.

MOROCCO. This large Berber "black tent" is used primarily during the summer season. It is divided by a curtain into two halves, one used for women and the other for men. A wide woven belt is tensioned over wood poles to support the tent.

AMERICA. American Indian nomadic tepees. Long poles lean into one another and are then wrapped with canvas. The traditional cover was buffalo skin.

MONGOL. Mongolian *gers*, also known as yurts in other areas. Felt covers a latticework of wood for the walls while the roof is formed by poles that meet at a compression ring. Each tent is occupied by one nuclear family. *(right)* Central skylight.

PAKISTAN. Tents made of modern lightweight materials used for a Japanese expedition of K-2 Mountain. Photographer Yoshio Komatsu was part of the team. These tents provided shelter for more than three weeks in the high winds and cold temperatures.

▲ ETHIOPIA. Thatched nomadic huts near the Kenya border.

▶ MOPTI, MALI. Moveable house made of tough, long rice straw, an original African variety that is commonly called "floating rice." In the rainy season, the rice heads grow on the surface of the river while the stalks and roots grow under the water. It is one of the three major rice types in the world—Japonica, Indica, and Graberima (floating) African rice.

NAMIBIA. Structures built of wood poles by the Himba people. They are covered with soil and cow dung for water protection. *(right)* The women paint themselves with red clay and oil.

BISBEE, ARIZONA. School bus converted into motorized shelter.

Natural
Conditioning

A MAJOR CHALLENGE facing all builders is that of constructing a building that is responsive to the extremes of the local climate. It can be difficult when using local materials and not having access to the abundant sources of energy needed for centralized heating and cooling systems. Other factors may also stand in the way of common sense, such as religious beliefs, existing building traditions, style and aesthetics, issues of durability, lack of other materials, and a lack of knowledge. The easy availability of other fuel sources such as timber in forested areas can reduce the incentive to explore other avenues despite the negative side effects of over-cutting.

Regardless of these limitations and hindrances, traditional builders in many parts of the world have demonstrated a great deal of ingenuity and common sense in designing buildings that rely upon natural conditioning. Most cultures have some means of achieving an improved microclimate around and within buildings. The most basic strategy is tied to reducing exposure to the harsh effects of climate such as sun, wind, rain, and snow. The design and shape of the building, careful site selection and improvement, building orientation, and the use of windbreaks and vegetation to improve ventilation are some of the methods that are utilized. Another important strategy is the use of seasonal and temporary climate modifiers such as screens and/or shields to reduce the effects of wind or to create shade. These function in the same way that a change of clothing allows the body to adjust to climatic changes.

▲ **PAKISTAN.** Wooden wind catchers.

◄ **THAILAND.** A small house with thatched porch. The hot air from the porch can escape out an opening in the gable end, which helps keep the house comfortable inside.

▲ **NEAR HYDERABAD, PAKISTAN.** Earth-covered wooden wind catchers, or *hawadans*, adorn rooftops. The use of wind catchers was dying out with the introduction of air conditioning. However, with the increased cost of electricity and frequent power outages, hawadans are once again becoming common.

Most buildings function effectively for at least part of the year, but there are climates that create comfort concerns throughout much of the year. In general, buildings are the most comfortable when several basic things happen. When the winter sun is allowed to enter the interior of the building on winter days, it stays much warmer. This is easiest when a large expanse of the building faces south. Controlling the entry of the summer sun, whether by overhangs of the roof or building under a south-facing cliff, is very effective. When ventilation is encouraged, especially at night in hotter climates, houses stay cooler and maintain a supply of fresh air. Wind scoops are one method that has been used to collect breezes above roof level and transmit them to the interior. Courtyards with vegetation and/or fountains are also used. Porches and verandas fulfill a variety of functions that include shading the walls, providing additional outdoor living space, and protecting the building from weather.

In many locations, it is advantageous to store heat or to cool the mass of the building to modify the interior climate. By taking advantage of the lack of heat in the night air, coolness is retained during the day. Heat generated during periods of cold is retained longer when there is sufficient mass. In contrast, where heat and humidity are more of a problem, traditional cultures encourage ventilation, making the house as open as possible.

▶ **ARDAKAN, IRAN.** The wind consistently blows from only one direction. The earthen houses in this hot desert all have earthen wind catchers, called *bad gir*, permanently built on the roofs facing the direction of the prevailing wind. They are designed with aerodynamic principles in mind as well as protection against sun to help keep the rooms and courtyards very cool.

JAISALMER, INDIA. These balconies overhang the streets below. The ornately carved yellow sandstone—"Haveli-style"—allows air and light to enter while preserving privacy by reducing visibility from the outside.

▲ **MATAM, SENEGAL.** The thatched porch protects this earthen bed that is used for sleeping outdoors. It is often cooler outside at night than inside. The earth wall has many small openings that allow for ventilation yet reduce the amount of sun that can enter.

▶ **SUIKHET, NEPAL.** A large thatch porch expands the living space of this oval-shaped wattle-and-daub house.

▲ **NEAR FES, MOROCCO.** Courtyard spaces create privacy and provide a balance of shaded and sunny areas. Houses can be oriented so that shadows on some of the walls create shade while allowing light to enter on others. Courtyards also allow for good ventilation yet provide protection from the wind.

◄ **BAISHA VILLAGE NEAR LIJIANG, CHINA.** Large verandas on both the ground level and upper story adjoin the courtyard spaces in Naxi.

Granaries,
Barns and Birds

IN ADDITION TO HOUSES and spiritual and public buildings, non-nomadic cultures require a class of building that supports their means of livelihood or sustenance. Since most of these societies are agrarian, the most common buildings to be found are those used for the storage and protection of grains, the processing of grain, and the care of livestock.

Of these, granaries are the most common, their forms and shapes varying as do the cultures where they are found. The more industrial the agriculture, the larger the granaries, such as the silos found in developed countries. The materials used for construction range from wood, vertical wooden poles, wattle and daub, and stone, to hand-formed clay. However, very large granaries are rarely built from earth, as there is a danger of collapse due to tremendous lateral pressure that grain exerts on the lower walls. As size increases, additional fiber reinforcement is needed.

Smaller granaries of many cultures are closely tied to pottery and basketry. The *cuezcomates* of southern Mexico are essentially large clay pots with thatched hats. Others use wattle-and-daub construction and are essentially a basketry technique in which everything is woven and tied. What is common to all granaries, regardless of where they are located, is that they are almost always unique and artistically crafted. Many approach the status of formal structures, while others are much more organic and playful in form. Most have floors raised above the earth and are set up on pillars, columns, and the like as a means of protecting them from rodents and other animals.

▲ NIOFOIN, CÔTE D'IVOIRE. Beautiful earth granaries with thatched roofs that are more than one hundred years old.

◄ TOGO. A Tamberma man placing a thatch cone on a granary.

The combination of legs/feet with other features creates unique shapes that often give them an appearance of living creatures.

Vital to agricultural life is the fertilization of fields. There are numerous places where certain birds are held in high esteem for their sources of manure and as an additional food resource in the form of meat or eggs. In the Middle East, towers are built to house the pigeons so that their droppings can be easily collected and distributed to the fields as manure. An average tower may house thousands of birds and produce thousands of pounds of fertilizer. The young that fall out of the nest are collected for food. Typically it is only the young that are eaten, as the older birds are needed for breeding stock and supplying manure. These pigeon towers are self-maintaining systems.

▶ LÉRÉ, CHAD. Grain is stored over the roofs of each room. Each wife has her own room. In this case, there are more than twenty wives. The wealthier the man, the more wives he has. Inside of each storage unit are three cavities sculpted from clay to divide millet, sorghum, and corn. They grow three varieties of grain so that if one has a bad year, there are two others on which to rely.

▲ **SAO VILLAGE, BURKINA FASO.** Square earthen granaries with wooden framework.

◄ **KSAR OULED SOLTANE, TUNISIA.** Vaulted storerooms for grain to be sold at the weekly market. Whenever more space is needed, another vault is added above like a wasp nest.

Granaries, Barns and Birds **303**

DOGON VILLAGE, MALI. Earthen granaries on stone pilings with flat roofs and thatched caps. There are often two types of granaries—one for men and one for women. Sometimes they are built under a cliff overhang for added protection.

CHAD. Earthen granaries with stone feet to keep animals out and to protect the base of the earth structure. Millet mats are used as hats to protect the domes. The structures on the far right are houses built from earth, then covered with a thick layer of wood as insulation.

▲ **NIAMTOUGOU, TOGO.** Small thatched granaries supported on pieces of stone slate.

◄ **BOUBON, NIGER.** Giant, domed, earth granaries built upon small stone feet. Crops are put in from the hole on the top and taken out from the lower part.

◄ **LOMBOK, INDONESIA.** Thatched granaries. Hanging bell–style granary behind. The upper part is used for grain storage while the large shaded area below is used as community social space for activities like weaving clothes.

▶ **MEXICO.** *Cuezcomates*—thatched granaries made from coils of clay and straw—are used to store corn.

▲ NORTHERN THAILAND. Thatched rice-straw storage.

◄ FADIOUT, SENEGAL. This village once lost all of its granaries to a fire. They are now built over the water for protection.

▲ BURKINA FASO. Temporary grain storage made from millet cane and millet mats.

► MOROCCO. Straw bales are kept dry by vaulting and plastering with earth. A drip edge is also built in.

◄ SULAWESI, INDONESIA. A rice granary with similar shape as a Tongkonan house.

ASTURIAS, SPAIN. Large wooden granaries are sometimes six to eight feet high. With four legs they are called *horreos*; with six legs, *paneras*.

▲ **LINDOSO, PORTUGAL.** Stone grain storage with a large stone between the post and base of the building for a rat guard.

▶ **SWISS ALPS, SWITZERLAND.** Wooden storage houses with stone rat guards.

▶▶ **LOFOTEN ISLANDS, NORWAY.** *Robuer*, a traditional fisherman's cabin made of wood. The gable-roof extension houses a pulley. The people here build nesting places for seagulls so they can easily collect their eggs.

NILE DELTA, EGYPT. Pigeon houses *(left)* and roosts made from stacked clay pots that are mortared together with mud *(below)*. These lightweight walls are earth-plastered and often lime-washed.

Pigeons are highly prized for their meat. They are very easy to keep since they hunt for themselves and unlike larger game animals, they are a more convenient size for feeding smaller numbers of people. Large amounts of manure are also collected and used as fertilizer in the agricultural fields. *(right)* Earthen pigeon houses.

TINOS ISLAND, GREECE. Dove houses built from stone. The lacy openings are where the doves enter and leave.

Communities,
Villages and Towns

TO COME TOGETHER in a community is a natural human pattern. Throughout time, communities have ranged from family clusters to large extended-family compounds, neighborhoods, villages, towns, and cities. We need and enjoy each other. As social beings we come together to gain advantages and to realize potential not possible as individuals.

Where, how, and in what form people come together depends on a complexity of factors that include everything from availability of water to richness of soils, availability of building materials, protection from enemies, favorable climatic conditions, cultural and spiritual beliefs, and the shape of the landscape. In the developed world, technology has brought about the ability to settle places that traditional societies could never consider. Armed with illusory self-sufficiency, it is now possible to ignore the constraints of the local environment and build whatever, wherever, and however we please. In many ways, the multiplicity of factors that need to be considered when choosing a location has been reduced to "a good view."

As populations increase and communities grow, there is a corresponding increase in the amount of infrastructure and resources needed to keep it all running. Towns and cities rapidly grow beyond the ability of their immediate context to support them, and ultimately they become dependent on goods and resources originating from places far removed. That dependency brings with it increased transportation and energy needs. And because the goods and products come from

▲ ANDALUCIA, SPAIN. Arcos de la Frontera village on upper Guadalete River. Villages near rivers were often built on higher ground for protection from floods and for the conservation of fertile lands for agriculture.

◄ ALONG THE ORINOCO RIVER, VENEZUELA. A circular Yanomami Indian structure called a *sabono*.

distant places, any harm or damage done to either the place or the local people usually goes unnoticed.

Urban sprawl, with is suburbs, shopping centers, and parking lots, relentlessly pushes nature farther and farther away until it becomes an abstraction—or even nonexistent—for most. The thirst and greed for more land reduces the surrounding landscape to flat and level ground capable of accepting the monotonous and repetitive architecture of the modern city. If not outward, then buildings grow upward. In modern apartments and high-rises, people are able to live totally self-contained, having very little if any contact with the actual ground.

If for no other reason than their size, people living in compounds, villages, and small towns are capable of fostering a sense of intimacy and stewardship for a place. This vital relationship also brings about a closeness and connection among those who live in proximity, as fundamentally stronger connections are formed when daily life is closely tied to the land.

▶ HABBAN, YEMEN. **South Arabian village**.

Placement

FROM ANCIENT TIMES, wherever a place was capable of supporting life, people settled. The landscape and natural context dictated where a community was possible. A perennial supply of water, soils for growing crops, and materials for building had to be present. The extremes of climate—high winds, floods, intense sun, or rain—had to be considered. When there was a concern for enemies, a site had to be defensible. In response to these factors, settlements can be found splaying out from the base of mountain ranges, nestled into caves formed by natural overhangs, contoured along hillsides, sitting atop plateaus, or lining the edges of rivers, lakes, or seas. In areas lacking sufficient resources for year-round living, nomadic lifestyles evolved.

For some cultures, a place needed to have spiritual significance or the correct "energy." The Pueblo Indians of the Southwest first needed to find "the center of the world" before it was seen as an appropriate place to settle. According to a Zuni story, "water spider and rainbow were asked to help determine the exact location of the village within the space of the four directional mountains. The people first went to water spider that spread his legs to the north and to the south, to the west and to the east. Water spider located the center of the earth directly under his belly. But the people wanted to be sure so they went to Rainbow. Rainbow stretched his bright arch to the north and to the south, to the west and to the east. He then confirmed water spider's place as being at the heart of the earth."

◄▼ CANYON DE CHELLY, NEW MEXICO.
Anasazi village.

▲ **VICOSOPRANO, SWITZERLAND.** Slate roof village in the Swiss Alps.

◄ **SHIMSAL VALLEY, PAKISTAN.** Village of stone houses set in the Karakoram mountain valley.

SETENIL, SPAIN. Set into the cliff, this village takes advantage of the natural protection.

AL-HAJJARA, YEMEN. Needing protection from enemies, this stone village was built as a fortress on top of the hill.

MONSANTO, PORTUGAL. Stone hillside village.

ACOMA, NEW MEXICO. "City in the sky"; plateaus, or *mesas* as they are called in the Southwest, provided easily defendable sites for villages.

▲ TINOS, GREECE. A whitewashed village on the edge of the Aegean Sea, with adjoining terraces.

◄ ANDALUCIA, SPAIN. Lime-washed village of Casares follows the contour of the hill.

Agriculture

WITH THE EXCEPTION of seafaring peoples, most permanent settlements are tied in some way to agriculture for their subsistence. For these settlements to sustain themselves over time, sufficiently rich soils were needed to support extended agricultural activity, as was dependable rainfall or water for irrigation.

Fertile soils and land that could be cultivated were highly regarded and rarely considered as building sites. Human settlement was placed where it would not interfere. Villages would be commonly nestled into the hills or on top of plateaus, leaving the fertile valleys below for agriculture. Where little more than mountainous hillsides existed, terraces were built to create areas for growing that could retain water and avoid erosion.

▲ TOYAMA PREFECTURE, JAPAN. Ainokura village. Terraced rice fields are in proximity to the village houses.

◄ LUZON, PHILLIPINES.
Ifugao people's thatched village surrounded by terraced rice fields.

▲ **NABUSIMAKE, COLOMBIA.** The Arhuaco Indians use this village of earth-thatched houses for community events. Village members also have additional houses in the mountains as well as near their agricultural fields.

◄ **TINERHIR, MOROCCO.** Earthen Kasbah village on the beginning of the Todra Gorge.

◄◄ **OLLANTAYTAMBO, PERU.** Set between Cuzco and Machu Picchu, this village is built primarily in the old Inca style. It is laid out on a rectangular grid following the valley. The equator-facing terraces near the outside edge of town receive ample sunlight, making it easy to grow crops. The sun hits the eyes of a large llama figure (upper corner) at the summer solstice, announcing the time to plant crops.

Community Form and Organization

THERE ARE NUMEROUS ways communities organize themselves. Sometimes this organization is the result of a very deliberate planning process that often produces formal and geometric shapes. At other times the process is casual and unintentional, where communities just grow over time as the context and conditions dictate. The resulting forms can range from pure chaos to a more organic organization, similar to the growth of a cell, where small distinct patterns repeat themselves over and over again, thus creating a whole. Since each pattern emerges out of a responsiveness to its surroundings, each is simultaneously the same and yet unique. Although repetitive, it is not boring or monotonous because it is not exact.

The forces that define a community's form are often the same ones influencing its placement. For example, in order to preserve agricultural land or to be more defensible, a village may be driven upwards or become more compact instead of low and sprawling. Perhaps a certain shape having symbolic meaning is incorporated into the overall community shape. The need for social and communal gathering places may dictate that buildings are added on or adjoined in such a way that usable exterior space is created.

For most traditional cultures, the local geography (or lay of the land) was something to which the placement and shapes of buildings had to conform. Local building materials, all with inherent characteristics, also mandated certain organization and form. Such strong determinates, often seen in our modern time as limiting and annoying, are exactly what give many traditional communities their character and charm.

▲ ORINOCO RIVER, VENEZUELA. An abandoned *sabono* along the Orinoco River, the main road of the area.

◄ CASAMANCE, SENEGAL. Thatched Eloubaline village organically clustered in the delta of the Casamance River near the Atlantic Ocean. The inverted roofs are for catching fresh rainwater, as nothing but saline water is available in the immediate area.

SHIBAM, YEMEN. These multistoried earthen towers are grouped in a compact rectangular form in Wadi Hadramaut. The tops of the towers are painted white to reflect the sun.

▲ ORINOCO RIVER, VENEZUELA. The Yanomami Indians build circular patterns of housing that sometimes form a complete structure called a *sabono*, as well as others that are made up of smaller units. These communities typically consist of about thirty people.

► FUJIAN, CHINA. Large family compounds, called *tulou*, are both circular and rectangular in form. Somewhere around 300 people inhabit these four-story structures. Each typically has two or three wells in the central space. *(inset)* Another type of *tulou* on a slope.

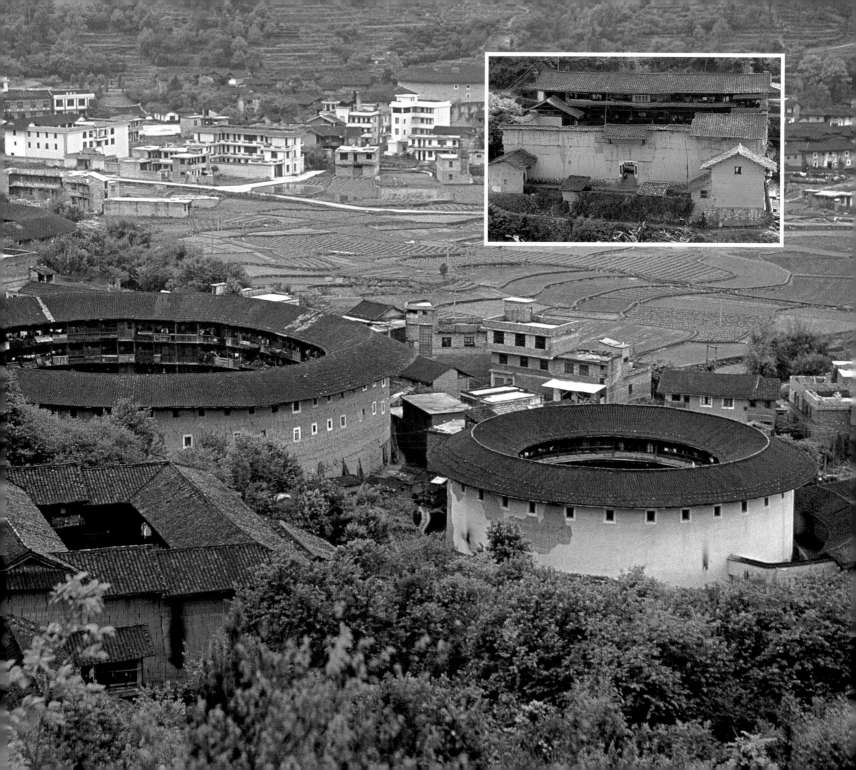

FUJIAN, CHINA. Interior of a large, circular, one-family compound. The diameter of this compound is 61 meters. There are more than 250 rooms in the four surrounding floors. The center of the first floor is for worshipping ancestors.

BORNEO ISLAND, MALAYSIA. Iban people's longhouse on stilts in Sarawak. Each row has about twenty rooms. Along its edge is a connected community space.

▲ **YAZD, IRAN.** A complex of earthen domes and vaults. The upper part of the lumps of earth seen in the background are the tracks of an underground waterway.

◄ **TANGASSOKO, BURKINA FASO.** Courtyard space created by connecting earth structures and walls.

▲ **NEAR FES, MOROCCO.** Family compound of adjoining earth structures, porches, and court-yards.

◄ **TAOS PUEBLO, NEW MEXICO.** Cluster built from earth bricks, or adobes, emulates the mountains in the background.

▼ **AGADEL, MOROCCO.** Village built from compacted, local clay soils blend into the surrounding land in the High Atlas Mountains.

▲ **ALBEROBELLO, ITALY.** Stone conical roofs of the Trulli houses.

▶ **DINKELSBÜHL, GERMANY.** Clustered roofs.

◀ **MATERA, ITALY.** This cave town in Basilicata completely covers the hill. Squatters sometimes occupy the old stone caves while new building continues right on top of them.

◀◀ **ANDALUCIA, SPAIN.** Hillside Casares village.

▲ FLORES, INDONESIA. Traditional thatch Ngada
houses in Bena village create a curving line.

◄ KONSO, ETHIOPIA. Thatched houses loosely
tucked in and around the dense vegetation.

Places of Worship

SINCE RELIGION IS such a vital part of cultures around the world, so are the structures where the people worship or pay homage. Shrines, churches, temples, mosques, and cathedrals are focal points not only for ceremonies but for many community social events and celebrations as well. The prominent part these buildings play in people's lives is often aggrandized by their prominent location, such as in the center of a village or on the top of a hill.

The more formal and organized the religion, regardless of the denomination, the larger and more formal the place of worship. Against its magnitude, surrounding houses and buildings can seem miniscule by comparison. And even when it is more modest in size, extensions such as towers or steeples then rise above all else, making it easily recognizable from a far-off distance.

In that they are seen as places of divine authority, the forms of these buildings mimic and surpass those associated with earthly governments and kings. They are often lavishly decorated and adorned with symbolic shapes, carvings, and painted designs. In order to denote that these structures are something different and unique, requiring special attention and respect, many are made to contrast sharply with the rest of the community. Sometimes this is accomplished by simply changing the color of the church or mosque from that of the other buildings in the village. Another effective means to declare contrast has been to use materials other than the local

MALI. Earthen mosque stands dominantly in the background.

ones, meaning that materials and skilled workers were brought in from far away, often at great expense.

Overall, places of worship seem to reflect the belief that God and the spiritual are not of this earth, but are superior and beyond the normal. Their fundamental pattern and growth is almost always upwards, as if striving to reach above everything and everyone, piercing the sky and pointing out the way to the heavens.

Perhaps the only exemption to this pattern is the kiva of the Pueblo Indians in the southwestern United States. This ceremonial place was built into the ground rather than above it, symbolizing the notion of going back into the earth; it was often referred to as a womb. Not only was this a place for ceremonial activities but for everyday community chores, such as grinding corn, weaving blankets, and consuming food. The spiritual was viewed as an integral part of nature and not distinct from everyday life. The kiva was not intended to be conspicuous but rather to remind people, through its understated sacredness, that they were part of the water and the wind/breath that flowed everywhere and through everything.

▶ SARAHAN, INDIA. Indo-Tibetan-style Bhimakali Temple, altitude 1,920 meters (6,299 feet).

◀ **OLVERA, SPAIN.** The large church blends into the red hills, contrasting with the white village below in Andalucia.

▶ **DOUIRETE, TUNISIA.** The village visually fades into the hill except for the lime-washed mosque. There is a graveyard in the foreground.

JIBLA, YEMEN. Praying in the courtyard of Queen Arwa Mosque.

◄ SAN JUAN OSTUNCALCO, GUATEMALA. Traditional folkloric dances in front of the church.

► KATMANDU, NEPAL. The gigantic Boudhanath Stupa.

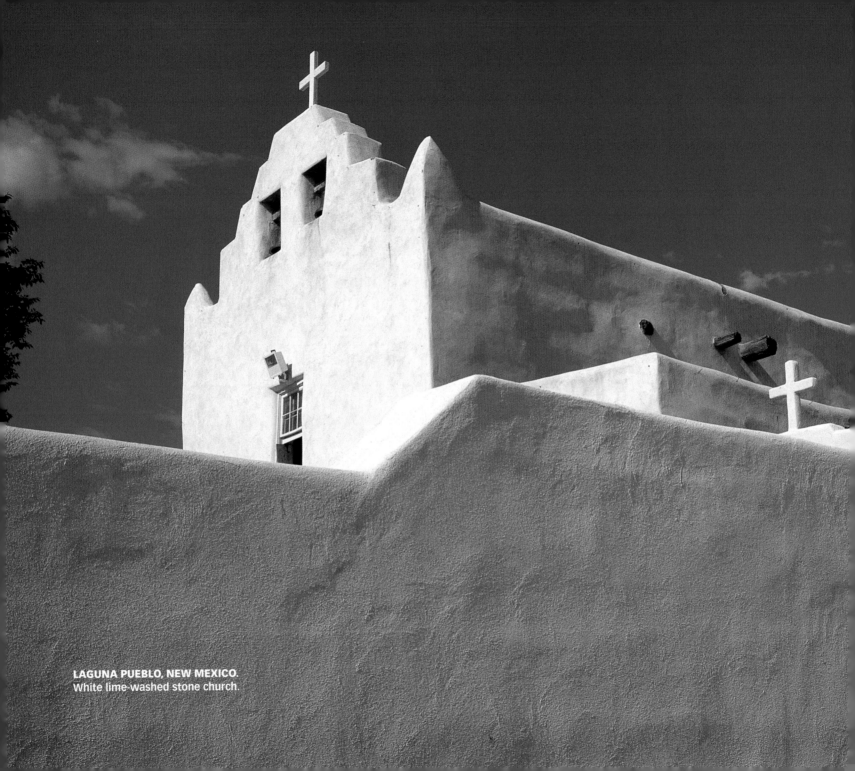

LAGUNA PUEBLO, NEW MEXICO.
White lime-washed stone church.

RANCHO DE TAOS, NEW MEXICO. Large adobe buttresses support the massive earth walls of the St. Francis of Assisi church. The highly sculptural rear portion of the church has captured the attention of artists and photographers worldwide. The local community gathers to renew the earth plaster on a yearly basis.

► **IRAQ.** Spiraling tower on an earthen mosque.

◄ **TIROL, AUSTRIA.** Church steeple reaches to the heavens.

◄ **BURKINA FASO.** This large mosque was built in a remote area, far from any settlement. Both the construction workers and materials were brought a long distance from Mali.

► **MALI.** This mosque made of earth sits in the midst of Dogon houses that are made of stone. Since there is no clay in Nando village, the material to build the mosque had to be brought from a distance.

▼ **KONG, CÔTE D'IVOIRE.** Earthen mosques are typically replastered with clay soils about every other year. Protruding wood beams are often built into the building and used as scaffolding during construction and plastering.

◀ BURKINA FASO. Earthen mosque.

▼ DJIGUIBOMBO, MALI. Dogon spiritual house used for the local religious authority.

▲ **NATAL, SOUTH AFRICA.** Zulu spiritual round house.

◄ **CÔTE D'IVOIRE.** Round mosque.

▲ HOLZGAU, AUSTRIA. Shrine ornately decorated with lime frescoes.

◄ MARAMURES, ROMANIA. Small household catholic shrine.

◀ **TOYAMA PREFECTURE, JAPAN.** Shintoism's small shrine.

▶ **KANINGRA, PAPUA NEW GUINEA.** A spiritual house made of sago palm along the Sepic River. These spiritual houses are called *haus tambaran*, a German word for "spirit." The term dates from the time when Papua New Guinea was a German colony.

▲ **MESA VERDE, COLORADO.** An Anasazi ceremonial kiva. Departing radically from the architectural forms that reach towards the heavens, this kiva is nestled into the ground, consistent with a belief system that saw deities as part of nature and the earth.

◄ **CÔTE D'IVOIRE.** The large stone is a place where people come to sacrifice chickens and pray for the safety of one's life.

ISTANBUL, TURKEY. A market street bustling with activity.

Streets

THE STREETS AND PATHWAYS of traditional villages and towns differ vastly from their modern counterparts. Today's urban centers are mostly stiff rectangular patterns organized around long, wide, repetitive corridors that facilitate motor vehicles getting from one place to another as quickly as possible. Nothing has come to dominate the layout and shape of today's cities more than the motor vehicle with the undeniable price tag of pollution, noise, congestion, and danger. A less obvious but equally negative cost is the isolation caused between people. Cars and trucks require space, whether stationary or moving. Cities become larger and more spread out. Destinations of work, home, and recreation are increasingly removed from one another with more people forever rushing to get there faster. In almost every respect, public life is spread thin, leaving people isolated within their own worlds, often inside their automobiles.

In traditional cultures the street is more than just a means of getting elsewhere; it is a destination in itself, a place where life happens. People can be found walking, conversing, even resting, with children playing and safely exploring the world around them. Flowers, trees, birds, and other signs of life are more common than not. Slower forms of transport are visible—bicycles, animals, carts, and people on foot. When present, motor vehicles simply are not dominant and often become extensions of the social space where people gather to sit, talk, or drink, whether parked in front of a house or in more public spaces. Places of activity line the streets,

AROUND FES, MOROCCO. **Walkway defined by reeds and the branches of a tree fence.**

from simple food stands, small cafes, public buildings, and churches to storefront businesses. As a street widens or converges with another, larger public spaces such as parks and plazas are formed, allowing for all types of ceremonial and informal gatherings and events.

Street surfaces vary from stone, brick, concrete, and grass to well-worn earth. Some are straight, others curved and undulating. Every turn harbors the potential of surprise. We change as the street changes, responding to different colors, patterns, textures, light, and shadow. We are thrilled by the excitement of a marketplace resplendent with colorful displays of fruits, vegetables, herbs, and local wares, and we find quietude and intimacy as we stroll down a narrow corridor arched with trellises and flowering vines.

Like veins in a body, streets can give vitality to a place. The daily life that moves through them is nourished and refreshed by the continual flow of activity, communication, energy, and people coming in and going out. Its networks of woven passageways connect a community to itself and the larger world outside.

◄ FUKUSHIMA PREFECTURE, JAPAN. **Thatched village divided in half by one main street. Post town in Ouchijyuku.**

► NIAS, INDONESIA. **The long, open space divides this Orihili village in half and serves as community space.**

◄ **TINOS, GREECE.** Narrow passageway between sculpted, lime washed walls.

► **GALICIA, SPAIN.** Penalba de Santiago village along the Camino de Santiago pilgrimage route.

▲ CASTLE COMBE, ENGLAND. Cotswolds region.

◄ PRAGUE, CZECHO. In the tradesmen's quarter are these tiny houses built into castle walls along the sixteenth-century "Golden Lane." A depression in the middle of the street allows for drainage.

▲ YUCATAN, MEXICO.

◄ CUNEN, GUATEMALA. A festival day.

▲ JAISALMER, INDIA. Multipurpose terraces right off the street serve as a well-used private space that is still connected to the public community. It is a place to chat with passersby. In the mornings the women use it to wash clothes. In the afternoon the elders may use it to take a nap. Because these daily activities aren't hidden away in more private spaces, the streets are kept alive. Jaisalmer was a camel-caravan city with constant traffic until sixty years ago when India and Pakistan were divided; the caravan route now cut by a border is isolated and dying.

◄ INLE LAKE, MYANMAR. Water market.

◄◄ **LEOMINSTER, ENGLAND.** The overhanging second floors on these Tudor-style buildings create a covered area for pedestrians below.

◄ **CAIRO, EGYPT.** The overhanging upper levels form a tunnel-like passageway.

Streets   **397**

◄◄ CARTAGENA, COLOMBIA. Lively arched palisades host numerous vendors, businesses, and public interactions.

◄ SUCRE, BOLIVIA. Long narrow trafficway slices through the colonial town.

▲ PRAGUE, CZECHO. An open-air cafe beneath a vaulted portal.

◄ VLKOLINEC, SLOVAKIA. Converging passageways join in the town square at the community well. It is a common place to meet and talk with others.

Entryways

AN ASTONISHING VARIETY of materials and techniques are used to distinguish or accentuate a door, entrance, or gate. Enhancements are added through colorful paint, carving, sculpting clay, plaster, or even elegant and complex carpentry. Sometimes the form, color, and symbol that are utilized have a deeper religious or symbolic significance. Others may be nothing more than an expression of personal creativity intended to create a desired mood.

Much of this decoration around doors is expressed by means of a molding or a thickening of the same materials that are used for the walls. Wherever an opening is made in a wall, the area surrounding it is weakened. By either thickening the same wall material or using a stronger material, then simultaneously an opening is reinforced and a molding is created.

Doors, gates, or the space around them have the potential to strongly impact those who approach, enter, pass through, or depart from them. Some create a sense of awe and grandeur; others convey peace and serenity. Bright colors may lift the spirit, while those that are dark and obscure may elicit caution, perhaps even tension. Often it is the area through which a person walks upon approaching a door or gate that accentuates the moment of transition. Curving walkways lined with plants or low-trellised walks are examples. It can even be the space that one encounters after having passed through an entrance that has the strongest influence. Changes of direction, views, levels, textures, colors, shapes, and angles all come into play.

▲ ETHIOPIA. Tree trunks form this entryway into a Konso family's compound.

◄ WALATA, MAURITANIA. Decorative frames painted and carved around door and window openings. The lime is painted on and then carved away.

For many traditional cultures, life is seen as a never-ending process of transition and is reflected in events such as the rites of passage or celebrations honoring the change from one season to another. In the same spirit, entryways, representing passages, are celebrated and honored. Sometimes they are purposely used to instill a heightened sense of awareness and respect. An example is the Japanese teahouse where the person entering is required to kneel down and crawl through a small opening, dramatically establishing that they have entered a different world.

In more industrialized homes and cities, doors remain unimaginatively the same virtually everywhere in the world. The act of entering a place—of moving from one place to another, from inside to out and outside to in—is a purely utilitarian act that requires no special care or attention, either physically, emotionally, or spiritually.

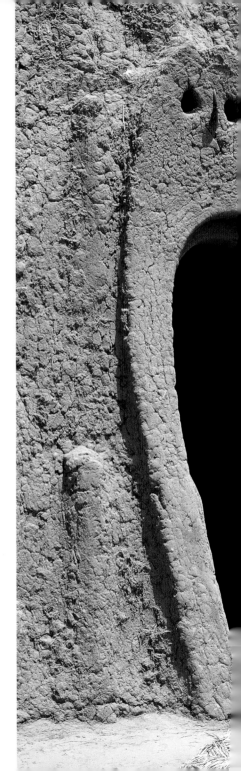

▶▶ **NORTHERN GHANA.** A low, protruding arched opening in Kassena's compound.

▶ **MOULA, CAMEROON.** Arched earthen doorway.

◀ **ZINDER, NIGER.** Decorative relief work done with lime plaster pronounces the entryway.

◄ **WALATA, MAURITANIA.** The white lime-wash molding strikingly contrasts against the dark earthen walls and makes the door opening look much larger. The three inset layers add a sense of depth to the entrance.

► **MATMATA, TUNISIA.** An arched lime-washed doorway to an underground house, framed by hanging clothes.

Built by Hand

◄◄ **MONSANTO, PORTUGAL.** Large white stones form a molding around this doorway. The sundial on the wall is also carved from stone.

◄ **AZTEC, NEW MEXICO.** This T-shaped doorway is often found in Anasazi ruins.

► **AL-HAJJARA, YEMEN.** The only entryway into the stone fortress village.

▲ GUARDA, SWITZERLAND. The rectangular
door is given an arched appearance by the
curving wall opening. The beveled walls also
make it appear larger. The fresco decorations
add a royal and playful touch.

◄ MONGOL. Brightly decorated door on this felt
ger, or yurt.

Entryways **411**

▲ BURKINA FASO. Children climbing over a low interior wall before passing through a low arched doorway. The low wall helps keep small animals as well as hot air out of the house.

◄ JAPAN. The traditional Japanese teahouse always has a low door that requires guests to kneel and bend down upon entering.

▲ **NGAOUNDÉRÉ, CAMEROON. Entrance to head chief's house,** "Lamido's palace."

▼ **SOUTH AFRICA**. Entrance to a round spiritual house in Zulu Land.

▶ **TLAXCALA, MEXICO**. Doorway in straw-thatched walls. *(bottom right)* **HIDALGO, MEXICO**. Doorway in house made from agave leaves

▶ **NIOFOIN, CÔTE D'IVOIRE**. A thatched entrance to an earthen Senufo people's village.

◀ **MARRAMLESH, ROMANIA**. Each house has a large entry gate. The larger doors are for horses and carts to pass through. The smaller carved entrance is for people.

Entryways **417**

Windows

LIGHT AND FRESH AIR filter through windows, which are the connection between the house and natural world. An approaching storm, bringing hopes of rain, might be announced by a sudden gust of wind swirling through the open window. Our spirits are replenished and nurtured as a room lights with the golden glow of the early morning sun, while the fragrance of window-box flowers drifts indoors.

Before the invasion of telephones, TVs, boom boxes, and computers into every household, windows were a critical communication link to the surrounding community. From windows, people quietly watched and felt the world around them. Leaning out an open window, people could hear the goings-on of the community, watch passersby, and casually talk to friends.

There is hardly a house that wouldn't benefit from the warmth of a low-angled winter sun shining through equator-facing windows. Or who wouldn't welcome the coolness of night air drifting through the house, removing the heat accumulated throughout the day. Carefully placed and sized windows can encourage breezes to enter where they otherwise might not. In hot climates, small and fewer windows create cavelike interiors that stay cool and dark, offering relief from extreme sunlight and heat.

The additions of shutters and/or curtains greatly improve a window's performance and add flexibility in meeting a variety of changing demands. Sometimes they may be needed to help keep out severe weather—rain, wind, cold, heat, or dust—

▲ YEMEN. Simple window with shutters in an earthen wall.

◄ CHITWAN, NEPAL. Window in a wattle-and-daub wall.

without sacrificing the light, air, or view. Screened latticework or blinds provide privacy by eliminating or reducing the view from the outside while simultaneously reducing harsh exterior light without blocking it completely.

On the exterior of a building, windows are often a strong defining element. Their location, shape, and size highly influence the appearance of a building, with personalities ranging from playful, sophisticated, and refined to rustic. Using attractive moldings, sculpting, finish carpentry, bright colors, and interesting details causes a window to stand out and catch our attention. Traditionally, many functional features, such as headers, lintels, sills, and eyebrows (used to keep water away) were beautifully and artistically incorporated. Like our own eyes, windows invariably reveal or suggest something about those within and become a natural place to add embellishment, contrast, and visual depth.

▲ BRETAGNE, FRANCE. **Window with flower box.**

▶ CICMANY, SLOVAKIA. **Strong geometric patterns painted with lime.**

ARDEZ, SWITZERLAND. Wooden shutters. The decorative frame around the window was done as *graffito,* an old Italian technique of painting with white and then scratching the surface to expose the color beneath.

▲ **MONSANTO, PORTUGAL.** Stone house and window built of natural rock.

▶ **AL-HAJJARA, YEMEN.** Lime-washed border around a window.

BHUTAN. *(top right)* A colorfully designed window.

▶▶ **FLORES, INDONESIA.** Window in a woven bamboo wall in Labuhanbajo village.

▲ GUARDA, SWITZERLAND. Beveled window openings with moldings created by using *graffito*. This technique remains in use in the Engadin Valley.

◄ GOLDEN RING, RUSSIA. Ornately carved wooden window moldings.

◄ **GUARDA, SWITZERLAND.** Playfully decorated wall and window moldings using fresco, a method where pigments mixed with water are painted directly onto freshly plastered lime.

► **WADI DHAHR, YEMEN.** Arched, stained-glass windows with decorative gypsum-plaster moldings.

▼ **FRANCE.** Mural creates a tree around windows.

Sculpted
Features

THERE IS AN undeniable elegance to a simple house that is free of modern clutter—excessive furniture, appliances, entertainment equipment, decorative décor, and knickknacks. In order to make these sterile, thin-shelled containers we call houses feel comfortable, we fill them with endless possessions. The flat, monotone surfaces we call walls need to be covered up and hidden with paintings, wall hangings, and the like because, in and of themselves, walls have no real beauty or substance.

When things such as furniture, shelves, stoves, or stairs are built right into a house, they innately feel very different from things that are mass-produced, purchased, and arbitrarily placed. Not only do they become expressively unique, having been built to match a specific context, but they can also transform a room into a place that feels equally special.

Shelves carved-in along a wall can add depth and interest. Benches sculpted in and around corners can soften the feeling of being inside a sharp-angled rectangular box. Stairways that are curved and contoured, at times narrow and sometimes twisting, can offer a much richer and intimate experience than climbing a normal flight of stairs.

A kind of "thickening" develops as these handcrafted extensions literally grow in and out from the edges of a room. The space becomes dynamic, alive with varying textures, light, and form, congruently blending grace and beauty with function to shape the everyday into something extraordinary.

▲ TIÉBÉLÉ, BURKINA FASO. Built-in earthen stairs, benches, and an earthen stove connect buildings and sculpt the exterior spaces. The woman is repairing with earthen clay.

◄ TINOS, GREECE. Lime-washed stone stairs.

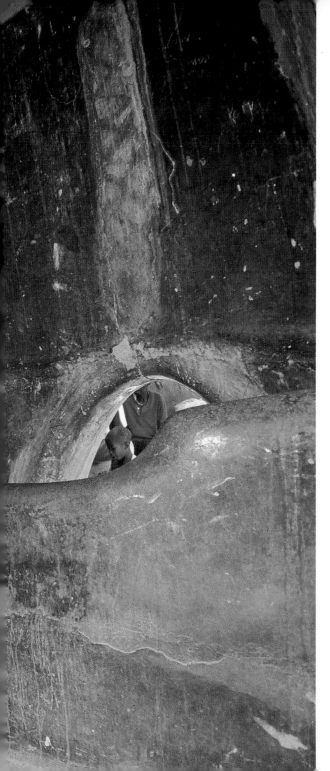

TANGASSOKO, BURKINA FASO. Built-in earthen seats, shelves, beds, and storage. The sculpted furniture and storage adds to the nonlinear surfaces. These rounded spaces with no corners are very soft and comfortable. *(left)* This is one of the wives' rooms. Men in Burkina Faso typically have four or five wives, and each wife has her own room. The small entrance to the left leads to an interior cooking room. *(above)* This serrated sideboard—called *chira yuga,* or "the face of the deceased"—holds the woman's collection of gourd utensils. It is molded from burnished clay.

▲ **NEAR JANAKPUR, NEPAL.** An earthen stove with two burners. Running around the wall is a Mithila design painted with clay.

BURKINA FASO. *(top right)* An earthen stove in the courtyard.

◄ **ZEBID, YEMEN.** Ornate shelves "nitched" into the wall and decorated with gypsum reliefs.

► **KINENKOUMOU, MAURITANIA.** Earth shelves built into walls and decorated with natural-colored clays by Soninke women.

▲ **WALATA, MAURITANIA.** Carved-in decorative niche. *(left)* Sculpted-clay bed and square earthen shelves set into a wall.

▶ **TANGASSOKO, BURKINA FASO.** Sculpted exterior earthen stairways.

▶▶ **CISTERNINO, ITALY.** Curving, lime-washed stone steps.

▲ JAISALMER, INDIA.

▶ MONSANTO, PORTUGAL.
Stone steps cantilevering out
of stone walls.

Embellishment

THE ASTONISHING DEGREE to which many traditional cultures embellish their homes and surroundings—even the simplest of structures—is a direct indication of the depth of connection and intimacy they have to their home and place. The hands of those who build, inhabit, and care for a dwelling can be readily seen and felt through the multitude of artistic touches. It is apparent that embellishment is not just an afterthought but rather a vital and necessary part of their lives.

When people, out of affection and care, make the things they create as beautiful as possible, the modern-day distinction between beauty and function is blurred. Even the most common, everyday, utilitarian items become works of art, such as a structural post carved with intricate detail or a simple entryway edged with lace-like designs.

Embellishment is recognized in many cultures as something that needs to be continually re-created, and is thus viewed as an opportunity to renew one's surroundings as well as oneself. When the natural pigments used to boldly decorate the exterior of a building are washed away with the rain, they are simply repainted without dread or regret, for it is acknowledged that in the act of creating beauty, the creator—as well as the creation—becomes enhanced and therefore more beautiful. Consequently, the process itself is valued as much, if not more, than the final product.

To decorate and embellish are not only artistic expressions but also powerful vehicles through which individual, cultural, and spiritual beliefs are conveyed. A

▲ **MALI.** Dogon's myth story carved into the wood panel of a door.

◄ **TIÉBÉLÉ, BURKINA FASO.** Woman decorates a wall with natural pigments.

pattern stained and woven into a bamboo wall may symbolically tell the story of who we are or where we came from, or a spiral relief sculpted onto an earthen wall may speak to us of our journey through life. Significant events are also commonly communicated. A historical battle or major political occurrence may be chipped into stone or depicted on a mural.

The modern industrial house lacks the embellishment that is so typical of traditional homes. The need, desire, and ability to express through the decoration of a dwelling rapidly diminishes as people become increasingly disassociated from the buildings they occupy and the places they live. In our transient culture, more and more people are renting and never even own their own homes, and those who do fall prey to a multiplicity of factors that keep them disconnected. Modern houses have become so large and complex that an army of tradespeople and specialists are required to build and maintain them. (The codes developed as protection from the outside hands of so many inevitably restrict and inhibit creative innovation or expression). Building materials have become so toxic and inflexible that interaction with them is arduous, and the tools and methods needed are beyond the skill and familiarity of most. Once completed, the perfection of the design discourages any change or modification. The fear of messing it up becomes paralyzing.

So we hire professionals to design and decorate inside and out. For beautification we buy artwork and décor made by someone else. And we allow the potential resale value to dictate the adornment and appearance of our home. In our commercial world, where time is money and so many things are reduced to a commodity, embellishment becomes a costly enterprise and is largely seen only as a luxury that most cannot afford.

BURKINA FASO. *(far left)* Decoration is done only by the women and only after a good harvest. It is very time-consuming. After painting, they polish the surface with a small stone. While they're working, they sing. If a woman doesn't decorate her house, the community perceives her as being very lazy. *(above)* Stone-polishing the surface seals it against moisture. White and black mineral pigments come from ground stone. *(left)* Clay is prepared to be used as a pigment.

◄ **NAVRONGO, GHANA.** After the rainy season washes all the paint off the houses, they are redecorated. Kassena house after being freshly painted. *(inset)* After the rainy season.

SOUTH AFRICA. Natural pigments are used to decorate walls with bold patterns.

PENSA·ANIMA·FIDELIS·
QVID·RESPONDERE·VELIS·
CHRISTO·VENTVRO·D·CCE

RENOVA 1972

99

DEVS·CVSTODIAT·INGRESSV

1647

DVMENG·CLALGVNA·
IVZI·ET·ION·CLAV·ET·IA
CHEN·SEIS·FILGS·A·1647·
QVID·SIS·QVID·FVERIS·QVIDERIS
SEMPR·MEDITERIS·
SIC·MINVS·ATQVE·MINVS·
PECCATIS·SVBYCIERIS·

▲ **HOLZGAU, AUSTRIA.** Fresco murals decorating the houses often tell stories of saints.

◄ **ARDEZ, SWITZERLAND.** The story of Adam and Eve is portrayed using fresco paint techniques on the walls of this old farmhouse.

▲ **VALLEDUPAR, COLOMBIA.** Painting a mural.

▶ **LUXOR, EGYPT.** The story of a pilgrimage to Mecca is painted on the wall. Guruna village stands on tombs of the nobles' ruins.

▲ NEAR JANAKPUR, NEPAL. Mithila clay and lime-
art painting tells a story.

◀ ETHIOPIA. Animals painted on the wall.

▲ CICMANY, SLOVAKIA. Geometric patterns painted with lime wash.

◄ AL-HAJJARA, YEMEN. Lime wash gives a lacelike decoration around the windows.

▶ **SIRIGU, GHANA.** Figures sculpted from clay.

◀ **ZINDER, NIGER.** Hausa lime plaster relief work.

TANGASSOKO, BURKINA FASO.
Snake and lizard figures sculpted with clay. Woman's space (left) and man's space (right) face the courtyard.

▲ **WALATA, MAURITANIA.** Arabesque-like interior-design work on whitewashed wall. Women paint with their fingers using clay pigments.

◄ **TIHAMAH, YEMEN.** Interior of a traditional thatched dome hut. The ceiling is decorated with the motif of a pilgrimage to Mecca, painted by a woman using her finger. The walls are adorned with a collection of many plates.

◄◄ **BHUTAN.** Mandala painted with natural paints.

GUJARAT, INDIA. Very ornate interior. Walls are clay reliefs with small, embedded mirrors.

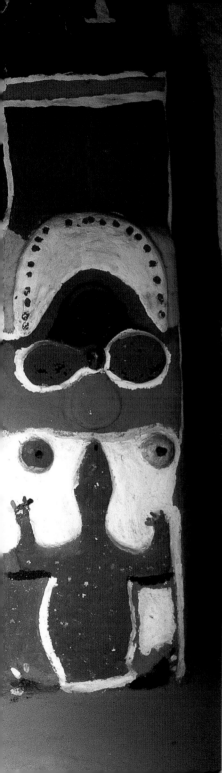

▲ **MAURITANIA.** The Soninke people in Kinenkoumou village enjoy painting their earthen houses with ornate designs. The women paint the walls with natural pigments after harvest.

◄ **NGAOUNDÉRÉ, CAMEROON.** Interior of Lamido's palace, decorated with natural clays and pigments.

◄◄ **SULAWESI, INDONESIA.** An intricate wood carving design under the protected gable-roof end of a Toradja's traditional house, called tongkonan. The pattern tells a story.

◄ **LIFU, NEW CALEDONIA.** A carved Melanesian totem pole is used as part of the chief's entrance gate.

► **SUMATRA, INDONESIA** The gable end of a roof in a Batak house in Lingga village is decorated with woven bamboo. The wood walls are decorated using ijuk rope to create symbolic designs of geckos.

Embellishment **465**

▲ **ALBEROBELLO, ITALY.** Stone conical-shaped dome roofs of "Trulli" houses, decorated with symbolic pattern. *(bottom right)* Painted with lime wash.

◄ **MARIB, YEMEN.** Stone decorations and ancient Sabaean script.

▲ CÔTE D'IVOIRE. Animals and dolls as fetishes, sculpted with clay on the wall of a spiritual house.

NEPAL. *(top right)* Engagement story.

► GHANA. Man and woman holding hands in a Kusasi interior.

►► NAMIBIA. A Himba woman grinds a red stone to be mixed with oil for body decoration. The people here regularly coat themselves with all types of oil, which makes them feel very comfortable.

Epilogue

I like to see houses in landscapes and natural environments. It has been my pleasure to experience these things in many parts of the world. Different shapes of house are temptations for me to photograph. When I find a beautiful house, my heart beats faster as I get feelings from its shape, materials and setting. Sometimes a house looks like a figure coming out of the earth. On the other hand, I also like to touch the ordinary lives of people who live in the house. They are always welcoming to me, in spite my appearing without forewarning or appointments. For these reasons, I travel a lot, anywhere in the world where I can encounter new impressive houses.

I have already visited many houses in the world, but there are still many houses that I would like to see. For example, a house on the very tall tree in Indonesia, a huge house with thatched roof in the Amazon, houses in a tiny little village on the edge of a mountain in Spain, a big granary made from clay in Niger.

Sometimes it seems I can find incredible houses by following my nose. When my wife, Eiko, and I visited one of Caribbean islands, my instinct told me there was something there for me. We rented a car to look all over the small island. Finally we came upon a small, impressive trapezoid house plastered with earth. The house had been used in the past for slaves working in plantation fields. Although it had a sad history, the house had a very nice form. The steadiness of its shape is a mixture of African, European and local cultures. On this island we found many houses of this style still in use.

There are many places I want to visit again. When I have the chance to go back, I will take pictures with me and hand to the people who live there. For the future, I will continue my world journey searching for and photographing wonderful new shapes in the landscape.

—Yoshio Komatsu

Bibliography

Bakewell, Anderson D., and Francine L. Stone. *Studies on the TIH_MAH*. England: Longman Group Limited, 1985.

Bourdier, Jean-Paul, and Trinh T. Minh-ha. *African Spaces: Designs for Living in Ipper Volta.* New York: African Publishing Company, 1985.

Carver, Norman F., Jr. *Iberian Villages: Portugal & Spain*. Michigan, Documan Press Ltd., 1981.

———. *North African Villages: Morocco/Algeria/ Tunisia*. Michigan: Documan Press Ltd., 1989.

Courtney-Clarke, Margaret. Foreword by Maya Angelou. *African Canvas: The Art of West African Woman*. New York: Rizzoli International Publications Inc., 1990.

Dawson, Barry, and John Gillow. *The Traditional Architecture of Indonesia*. London: Thames and Hudson Ltd., 1994.

di Muro, Edoardo. *Afrique*. Italy: Hatier 5 Continents, 1990.

Gil, Júlio, and Augusto Cabrita. *The Loveliest Towns and Villages in Portugal*. Lisbon/São Paulo: Editorial Verbo, 1991.

Goldfinger, Myron. *Village in the Sun: Mediterranean Community Architecture*. New York: Rizzoli International Publications Inc., 1993.

Guidoni, Enrico. *Primitive Architecture: History of World Architecture*. New York: Rizzoli, 1987.

"GA Houses" No. 54, 56, 57. Tokyo: ADA Edita Tokyo Co., Ltd.

Kamiya, Takeo. *The Guide to the Architecture of the Indian Subcontinent*. Tokyo: TOTO Ltd., 1996.

Kawashima, Chuji. *Sekai no Minka*. Tokyo: Sagami Shobo, 1990.

Komatsu, Yoshio. *Living on Earth*. Tokyo: Fukuinkan Shoten Publishers Inc., 1999,

———. Life on Earth. Tokyo: Fukuinnkan Shoten Publishers Inc., 2001.

Minzoku-Gaku Ouarterly. Osaka: Sennri Foundation.

Ohta, Kunio. *Wooden Architecture in Europe.* Tokyo: Koudannsha, 1985.

Primitive Worlds: People Lost in Time. Washington D.C.: National Geographic Society, 1973.

Shelter. California: Shelter Publications, Inc., 1973.

Steele, James. *An Architecture for People: The Complete Works of Hassan Fathy.* New York: Whitey Library of Design, 1997.

Taylor, John S. Translated by Hisashi Goto. *Commonsense Architecture.* Tokyo: Shokokusha, 1989.

Yagi, Koji . *A Japanese Touch for Your Home.* Tokyo/New York/San Francisco: Kodansha International Ltd., 1982.

Yampolsky, Mariana. Text by Chloë Sayer. *The Traditional Architecuture of Mexico.* London: Thames and Hudson Ltd., 1993.